Just Right Words

SLAM Poetry

Elizabeth Siris Winchester

Consultants

Kenn Nesbitt
Children's Poet Laureate 2013–15

Publishing Credits

Rachelle Cracchiolo, M.S.Ed., *Publisher*
Conni Medina, M.A.Ed., *Managing Editor*
Nika Fabienke, Ed.D., *Series Developer*
June Kikuchi, *Content Director*
John Leach, *Assistant Editor*
Lee Aucoin, *Senior Graphic Designer*

TIME For Kids and the TIME For Kids logo are registered trademarks of TIME Inc. Used under license.

Image Credits: Cover and p.1 Michael Loccisano/Getty Images for Mad Over You; Reader's Guide page Derek Davis/Portland Press Herald via Getty Images; pp.4, 5 Bennett Raglin/Getty Images for DreamYard Project; p.6 dpa picture alliance/Alamy Stock Photo; p.7 Christian K. Lee/The Washington Post via Getty Images; p.8 Patrick Farrell/Miami Herald/MCT via Getty Images; p.9 Tim Mosenfelder/Getty Images; p.13 Philip Scalia/Alamy Stock Photo; p.14 ZUMA Press, Inc./Alamy Stock Photo; pp.14–15 Jonathan Newton/The Washington Post via Getty Images; p.16 Dimitrios Kambouris/Getty Images for Tony Awards Productions; pp.16–17 Yoon S. Byun/The Boston Globe via Getty Images; pp.18–19, 21 Bennett Raglin/Getty Images for DreamYard Project; p.23 Michael Loccisano/Getty Images for Mad Over You; p.27 Patrick Farrell/Miami Herald/MCT via Getty Images; p.31 Barry Chin/The Boston Globe via Getty Images; all other images from iStock and/or Shutterstock.

Teacher Created Materials
5301 Oceanus Drive
Huntington Beach, CA 92649-1030
http://www.tcmpub.com
ISBN 978-1-4258-4981-8
© 2018 Teacher Created Materials, Inc.
Made in China
Nordica.072017.CA21700822

Table of Contents

It's a Poetry Slam!

Slam poetry is a form of spoken word poetry. People write and perform it for others. But slam poets don't wear costumes or use **props** or music. Some poems have a **rhythmic** or musical sound when read aloud. Other poems don't.

Slam poets use words to express thoughts and make people feel something. Their words are powerful. Slam poetry is often about the author's identity, including his or her **race** or gender. Or it can be fun and silly.

There are rules for slam poetry competitions, known as *poetry slams*. But there are few rules for writing the actual poems. Slam poets write about anything. They use words as they wish and do not need to follow the usual grammar rules.

Students perform onstage at the Bronx-Wide Poetry Slam Finals.

About ME

Momma told me to know my story
She said, "Learn you and tell the world as you do"
To dream 3-point shots
but shoot to read everything
& give everything all you got
She warned about his stories found in schoolbooks given to me
Said be ready cause barely anyone in there will look like me
Think like me Like me
Then I found Poetry
Poetry like me
So I started writing
Started writing about me
About What I wanted to see
How I wanted to believe
In who I was to be
So I started writing to learn about me
ME

—½ Pint Poetics,
   Ravenswood
   Elementary School
   fifth graders,
   Chicago, Illinois

Write On!

People have always told stories. Poetry is one way to do so. A construction worker and poet named Marc Kelly Smith came up with a new way to share poetry with others. Smith started the poetry slam **movement**.

Smith felt that poets should be free to *not* follow rules. He thought poetry had lost its passion. In 1986, he started a weekly poetry reading. It was at a jazz club in Chicago, Illinois. His readings became popular. Smith hosted the first poetry slam at another Chicago jazz club. In poetry slams, judges from the audience score the poets. The scores are based on the writing and performance of the poetry.

Rhythmic Writers

Langston Hughes (LANG-stuhn HYOOZ) was an American poet. He wrote "jazz poetry." It had rhythms similar to the ones in blues and jazz music of the time.

Jordan Perry, 17, recites one of his poems in front of the Martin Luther King Jr. Memorial.

Slam poetry and poetry slams quickly spread across the United States. Slam poets shared their work in cafés and clubs. They read at open mic nights. These are events where inexperienced people perform for an audience. Anyone can go on stage to sing, tell jokes, perform poetry, and more. Slam poetry spread to other countries, too. Younger writers began to take part. In 1990, the first National Poetry Slam took place. It was held in San Francisco, California.

James Kass helped bring slam poetry to teens. He started the group Youth Speaks in 1996. Other groups teach slam poetry to elementary school kids.

That Rules!

Poetry slam rules can vary, but these are common:

- Poets compete as individuals or on teams.
- Poets must perform poems that they wrote themselves.
- Poets get three minutes to read one poem.
- Costumes, props, and instruments are not allowed.
- Judges are chosen from the audience. They give scores to the poets, which are used to figure out who competes in the next rounds and who wins.

James Kass (center) and Youth Speaks poets attend a premiere party for HBO's *Brave New Voices* and Youth Speaks in San Francisco, California.

TV Time

A television show that aired for five years also helped make slam poetry popular. It was called *Def Poetry Jam*. It allowed people to watch slam poets in action.

Earth Day

Trash on the ground ends up in the sea.
People use too much electricity.
Careless people leak oil into the sea
    like it was a dumpster.
All of this is starting to destroy her.
People pollute the air with their cars.
We don't want to end up like Mars.
People use way too much paper.
Global warming is making water into vapor.
Here's the problem: too much pollution.
Reduce, reuse, recycle is the solution.
We are like a **tsunami** washing away the earth.
Don't you think it hurts?
So these are some things we all can do

To stop making the earth feel blue.
1. Recycle more and throw out less trash.
2. Use less electricity by turning off the lights that
    are not in use.
3. Don't drive, instead bike or walk.
4. Use less paper cause it's wasting trees.
Make sure you do all of these.
Save the earth! Save the earth! Save the earth!
Don't be mean, be green!

—½ Pint Poetics, Lara Elementary
    Academy second graders,
    Chicago, Illinois

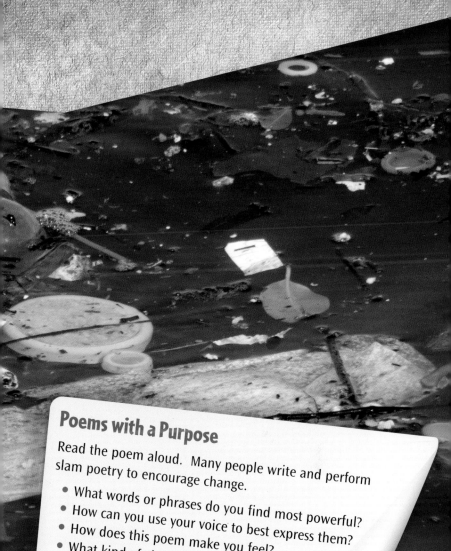

Poems with a Purpose

Read the poem aloud. Many people write and perform slam poetry to encourage change.

- What words or phrases do you find most powerful?
- How can you use your voice to best express them?
- How does this poem make you feel?
- What kind of change do these poets hope to bring about?
- Why do you think the authors wrote the poem?

Word Warriors

The Nuyorican (new-yo-REEK-in) Poets Cafe is in New York City. It opened in 1973. A group of Puerto Rican writers started it. The café is known for its open mic nights and Friday night poetry slams. Top poets compete in the Friday slams. People wait in lines to listen to slam poets.

Top performers can join the café's National Poetry Slam team. Groups from all over the United States compete in this event. People can compete in a group or perform **solo**. The café has other programs for poets, musicians, and actors of all ages.

Get to Work

The Nuyorican sometimes holds poetry slam **workshops** for kids. The workshops start with a performance by poets. Then, the students are placed in small groups so they can write about their own experiences.

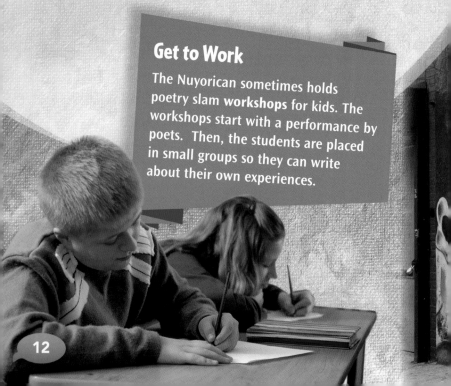

Poetry of the People

"Slam poetry events involve a lot of **interaction**," Daniel Gallant explains. He is the Nuyorican's executive director. "Slam poets rely on energy from the audience."

Poets in Chicago

Kuumba Lynx (KOOM-buh LIHNKS) is an urban arts youth group in Chicago. It was founded by Jaquanda Villegas (juh-KWAN-duh vee-YEY-guhs) and Jacinda Bullie (hah-SIHN-duh BUL-ee) more than 20 years ago. The group provides a safe place where teens can express their thoughts. In the group, teens connect with poetry through the use of hip-hop. Villegas says, "Like the **MC** in hip-hop, the slam poet has the power to move the crowd!"

STOP! THINK...

This photo shows a teen performing for an audience at a poetry slam.

> What emotions do you think the poet is feeling?

> What clues in the photo give you an idea of how the poet might feel?

> What do you think the poem could be about?

In 2008, the group started a program for kids ages 8 to 14. It is called ½ Pint Poetics. Kids are taught to think and write about "class, race, gender, and global impact," says Bullie. School teams take part in a poetry slam each year. The slam ends with a hip-hop concert.

High school student Kyle Taylor hosts a regular poetry slam at his school.

Poets in San Francisco

Youth Speaks is based in San Francisco. It is for people ages 13 to 24. The group has programs across the country and around the world. It created the first national youth poetry slam in 1997. This event is called Brave New Voices. It takes place in a different U.S. city every year.

"We think every young person has a voice, and we want to work with youth to find their voice and present it," says Kass. "I started Youth Speaks to give young people a space to define who they are."

He Diggs It!

The hip-hop musical *Hamilton* is a Broadway smash hit. Daveed (dah-VEED) Diggs won a Tony Award® for playing the roles of Thomas Jefferson and the Marquis de Lafayette (mahr-KEE duh lah-fah-YEHT). He took part in Youth Speaks when he was in high school. He says poetry slams are the reason for his success.

Teens Talk

"I knew how much writing meant to me when I was young," Kass says. He suggests that kids watch slam poetry videos and see it live. "The most important thing is to be yourself and have fun."

You're a Poet, You Know It!

"Spoken word poetry is the art of performance poetry. It involves creating poetry that doesn't just want to sit on paper. Something about it demands it be heard out loud," says Sarah Kay.

Kay was in a poetry group in college with another student named Phil Kaye. Together, they started Project VOICE. The group teaches kids in all grades about spoken word poetry. The group has worked with hundreds of schools in over 20 countries.

Sarah writes poems to figure things out. Phil likes writing and sharing poems with others. Think about the words and meanings of this poem as you read it.
Say it aloud, with feeling.

DreamYard Project hosted the Bronx-Wide Poetry Slam in 2016.

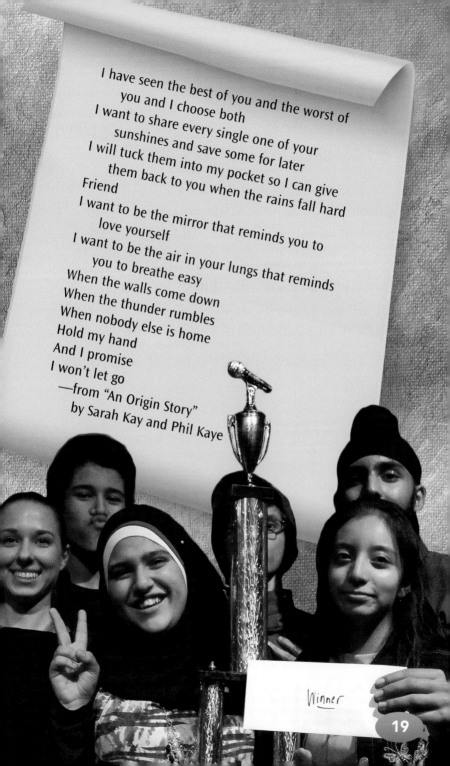

I have seen the best of you and the worst of
you and I choose both
I want to share every single one of your
sunshines and save some for later
I will tuck them into my pocket so I can give
them back to you when the rains fall hard
Friend
I want to be the mirror that reminds you to
love yourself
I want to be the air in your lungs that reminds
you to breathe easy
When the walls come down
When the thunder rumbles
When nobody else is home
Hold my hand
And I promise
I won't let go
—from "An Origin Story"
by Sarah Kay and Phil Kaye

Winner

19

Phil Kaye found slam poetry in high school. "I thought poetry was something I didn't like until I saw someone…perform a spoken word poem," he says. "I still remember feeling, 'Wow! I can't believe this is something I'm allowed to do.'"

Project VOICE helps kids start writing with three big questions: What do I write about? How do I write about it? How do I perform it?

"Poetry doesn't necessarily have to be about a big, huge moment that makes you cry. It can be about a tiny thing," explains Kaye. "We have a million thoughts and ideas every day."

Use these two exercises to put your thoughts on paper!

Exercise 1: List It!

Make a list of three things you know to be true. The only rules are to use details and to not think too hard. For example, Kaye likes the Los Angeles Lakers, Friday afternoons, and chili. Kaye might say he likes chili because when he was little, his dad used to make it with him.

Exercise 2: Use Your Voice

Sometimes, spoken word poets use their voice to give their poems a musical quality. Sometimes, poets whisper. Other times, they speak loudly. Experiment with the **tone**, **pitch**, and volume of your voice. You can use these tools to share your poem in a way that feels right to you.

Poetry Rules!

There are three main categories of poetry. Lyric poems tell a person's thoughts or feelings. Narrative poetry tells a story. Dramatic poems use characters to act out a story. Each of these categories includes many forms of poems. Slam poetry is a form of lyric poetry.

When it comes to writing, slam poetry doesn't have any rules. But other types require poets to follow rules. For example, haiku has a certain number of syllables and lines. Other poems have rhyme patterns.

All poems are creative ways for people to express themselves. Rhythm is the way the language flows and sounds in a poem. Poetry often includes patterns known as *meter*.

Haiku

This Japanese poetry form has 17 syllables that are broken up into three lines. The first and third lines have five syllables. The second line has seven syllables. The poem often includes a word that tells or hints at the season the poet is writing about.

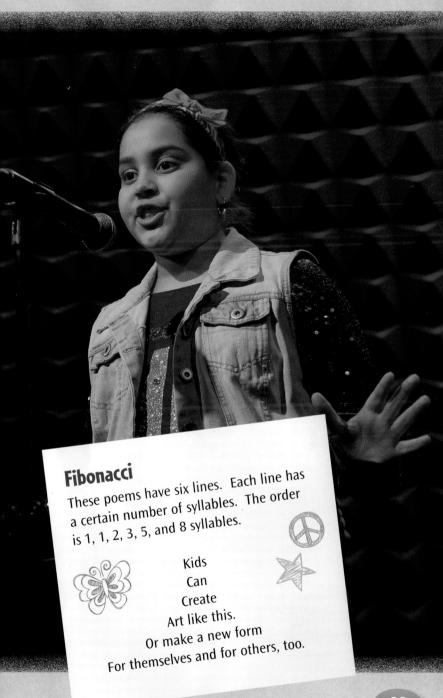

Fibonacci

These poems have six lines. Each line has a certain number of syllables. The order is 1, 1, 2, 3, 5, and 8 syllables.

Kids
Can
Create
Art like this.
Or make a new form
For themselves and for others, too.

How to Throw a Poetry Slam

½ Pint Poetics offers these tips for getting started:

🔊 Gather a crew of teachers, artists, students, and community members.

🔊 Get kids interested by having a slam poetry performance at a school assembly. Afterward, have students sign up to take part in a poetry slam.

🔊 Decide whether you will have a slam team or individual poets.

🔊 Classes could compete against each other, or school against school. Or kids could perform as individuals.

🔊 Structure the slam in a way that lessens competition. Celebrate strengths.

🔊 Figure out details. Who will compete? When and where will the slam take place? How will you invite the community?

🔊 Record the event. Find someone to take pictures and make a video.

🔊 Make it fun with food, giveaways, judges, hosts, a DJ (to play music between poems), and a full audience. Make sure participants know the rules of the poetry slam. The goal is for everyone to exchange ideas and have fun!

Find Your Voice

The sun rises. It's time to get out of bed.
Your mom rushing you along
    is something you dread.
Instead of getting angry, think about
    all there is to see and do
What exciting things might happen to you?
Write them down, you never know just
    where your thoughts might let you go!

Why not give slam poetry a try? Use the information throughout this book to help you get started. Remember that there are no rules for writing slam poetry. Find your voice and be real. "A writer is someone who thinks and has ideas about the world," says Jacinda Bullie of Kuumba Lynx. "We're all writers. Some just haven't put their thoughts on paper yet.

A Winning Writer

In 2012, Santino Panzica won the TFK Poetry Contest. Santino was only 12 when he won! The next year, he published his first book of poems. It is called *The Man-Eating Lemon*.

Contest Time

TIME For Kids holds an annual poetry contest. It is open to kids ages 8 to 13 in the United States. Kids can write and send in poems that are funny and rhyme. They must be original and not copy another poet's work.

Glossary

interaction—when people communicate or react to each other

MC—short for *master of ceremonies*; the person in charge of the microphone

movement—a series of acts working toward an end

pitch—a quality of sound that can be high or low

props—objects used by performers to create a certain effect

race—belonging to a group of people with the same ancestry

rhythmic—having a pattern of sounds or movements

solo—alone

tone—quality of spoken sound

tsunami—a large sea wave caused by an earthquake, volcano, or other changes underwater

workshops—educational meetings or discussions that allow people to learn about or explore a specific topic

Index

Check It Out!

Books

Regan, Dian Curtis. 2010. *Barnyard Slam*. Holiday House.

Swados, Elizabeth. 2002. *Hey You! C'mere! A Poetry Slam*. Arthur A. Levine Books.

Videos

LPS Media. *Wetherbee 3rd and 4th Grade Poetry Slam*.

Mali, Taylor. *On Girls Lending Pens*.

MentorTEAM. *Mentor Grade 6 Poetry Slam!*

Project VOICE. *An Origin Story*.

TED-Ed. *Miss Gayle's 5 Steps to Slam Poetry*.

THNKR. *Kioni "Popcorn" Marshall: Prodigy Poet*.

Websites

½ Pint Poetics. www.kuumbalynx.com/half-pint-poetics-2/.

Nuyorican Poets Cafe. www.nuyorican.org.

Project VOICE. www.projectvoice.co.

Youth Speaks. www.youthspeaks.org.

Try It!

Perform your poetry! Imagine that your school is hosting a poetry slam and needs kids to take part. You accept the challenge.

🔊 What will you write about?

🔊 Will your poem focus on a small moment or a big idea?

🔊 Use some of the tips in this book to get started. Share your poem with a friend.

🔊 Practice performing. Slam poets play with their voice to get their message across. You could whisper, yell, or even break into song.

Poem

I just got home from work
To find no food
My stomach empty
While you have plenty
I am poor
You have much more
than you need
—Caroline W.,
grade 3, Sea Cliff, NY

About the Author

Elizabeth Siris Winchester has written for *TIME FOR KIDS* for almost 20 years. She has covered a range of topics from bullying, bats, and butterflies to amazing kids and groundbreaking figures. She is grateful to have found work that she enjoys and finds meaningful. She thanks her three kids for inspiring her often. She also loves running, yoga, baking, music, dogs, and especially time with friends and family.

DARWIN'S VISION AND CHRISTIAN PERSPECTIVES

Edited with an Introduction by
WALTER J. ONG, S.J.

and a Foreword by
JOHN WRIGHT, D.D., Bishop of Pittsburgh

New York THE MACMILLAN COMPANY 1960

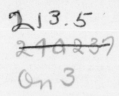

Imprimi potest   Joseph P. Fisher, S.J.
St. Louis, Missouri   Provincial, Missouri Province
March 30, 1960

Nihil obstat   William M. Drumm
                                        Censor Librorum

Imprimatur   ✠ Joseph E. Ritter
St. Louis, Missouri   Archbishop of St. Louis
April 12, 1960

© The Macmillan Company 1959, 1960

First Printing

The Macmillan Company, New York
Brett-Macmillan Ltd., Galt, Ontario   3849

Printed in the United States of America

Library of Congress catalog card number: 60-14486

FOREWORD

Ideas, true or false, continually revolutionize human history. No chain reactions set off by explosions in the world of matter have effects in space or time so far-reaching as the chain reactions set off by ideas in the world of the intellect.

Human history in the last century has been profoundly influenced, even modified in amazing measure by chemistry, physics and the material explosions which these have made possible. We already know something of the revolutionary effects, good and evil, of the newly discovered laws at work in matter as these are revealed in medicine, communications, warfare, industry and technology; we have yet to learn of the long-range effects of radioactive fallout and other forces let loose in the realm of material energy.

Ideas are even more devastating or more beneficent in their revolutionary effects than these physical forces. In recent generations certain master ideas have been of far greater influence in shaping the history of our times than have the most astonishing physical prodigies.

Three controversial ideas have particularly revolutionized the thinking of our times and have affected the content and direction of our civilization. The influence of these three ideas has been universal, radical and permanent; no one in civilized society can possibly have escaped the changes made inevitable in human history by these concepts. They have directly modified and revised the attitudes, values, institutions and conduct of the millions who have accepted them in whatever degree; they have indirectly caused or occasioned modifications in other millions who have been greatly challenged by them, even though these millions may have subsequently rejected, summarily or in substantial part, the ideas in question.

These ideas are, of course, the ideas associated with the names of Marx, Freud and Darwin. If the physical world has been tremendously changed by electronics, nuclear science and technology during these last hundred years, that change is as nothing to the revolutions brought to pass in the intellectual world by the ideas of these three men.

The *philosophia perennis* of Christendom and, more especially, the theological science which has developed out of and around the Christian faith have inevitably encountered these revolutionary thinkers and undertaken to measure the value of the ideas emanating from them. These estimates have not been equally easy, nor have the judgments been equally final. The thinking of Christendom has felt the impact of all three. It has profited from valid insights gained as a result of speculation on each and from the revision of certain traditional emphases as a result of lessons learned in the light of both the error and the truth highlighted in the controversies surrounding these three names and the ideas associated with them. Christian publications, debates and disputations have piled up bibliographies on the ideas launched by Marx, Freud and Darwin; these are in themselves impressive evidence of the impact these ideas have had on the scholars and the interests of Christendom.

The ideas promulgated by Karl Marx have been closely identified with the practical order of the daily lives of men and nations. As a result, they have been analyzed and evaluated with relative ease. The brutalities of atheistic Communism and the crudities of dialectical materialism have made relatively facile the refutation of the master ideas of Marx; no ecclesiastical condemnation or philosophical rebuttal of Marxism exposes its essential errors more clearly or more cogently than does the experience of its pragmatic results and the practical corollaries of its cynicism.

The idea of Freud, directly concerned with the mind and even the soul rather than with the practical order of economics and politics, has been much more elusive. The critique of his theory by the Church and its evaluation by Christian scholars have been more tentative, cautious and qualified. Where condemnation has been required by faith or reason, it has been swift and sure, but always addressed to specific errors rather than the total system of ideas. No one speaking authoritatively for the Church or responsibly for Christian scholarship has been moved to make so sweeping a rejection of the master idea of Freud as Pope Pius XI made of Marxism when he labeled Communism as intrinsically perverse, so totally false that no one could assimilate any part of its essential tenets and retain the name of Christian.

The final judgment on the revolutionary ideas of Freud will probably find Freud's own statement of his theories largely unacceptable to Christian faith or philosophy, but will not less probably find both faith and philosophy greatly illumined, even confirmed by the speculations and conclusions of those impelled by Freudianism to explore anew and more deeply the nature of man, a creature composed of body and soul and made in the image and likeness of God.

Like observations might be made about the idea launched by Charles Darwin just over a century ago. The concept of evolution, even more than that of Marx's materialism or the postulates of Freudianism, has dominated the intellectual world during the past century. It would take an encyclopedia to recount the scientific, philosophical, sociological and theological questions which have been raised and clarified or complicated by the idea of evolution. Here, too, the authentic mind of the Church and the sober reactions of Christian scholarship have been characterized by critical caution and careful effort to differentiate truth from half-truth or flat error and to salvage solid science from fanciful or fallacious speculation.

Again, one may well contrast with Pius XI's total rejection of the Communist idea the manner in which our Late Holy Father, Pope Pius XII, called attention in the encyclical *Humani Generis* to the need for scholarly discussion of the issues concerned with cosmic and organic evolution, issues arising from the master idea of Darwin.

The present volume of papers by Catholic scholars is an attempt to contribute to such scholarly discussion. These papers are in no sense pamphlet refutations of Darwinism; neither are they naive efforts at uncritical assimilation into Catholic thought of the postulates or corollaries of Darwin's master idea of evolution. These Catholic theologians, philosophers and scientific scholars do not pretend to have written a final synthesis of Darwinian conjecture and Catholic dogma. Their essays are not offered as the judgment which the Church and her scholars will eventually make on the fact and full implications of evolution. They have merely attempted, from the vantage point afforded by a century of intellectual chain reactions set up by Darwin's idea of evolution, to take tentative measure of that idea by norms which Catholic scholars find pertinent.

The undersigned is unprepared to evaluate the accuracy of some of their measurements or the validity of all their conclusions. He notes that these are, as they should be, tentative and cautious. But the spirit and motivation of this scholarly discussion one can only welcome with praise and gratitude. After all, even Darwin confessed that "the mystery of the beginnings of all things is insoluble to us." Such an acknowledgment invites theologians and philosophers to make their comments, with great sobriety and humility, on that idea of evolution by which Darwin, however valid his own hypotheses, indubitably gave new and revolutionary direction to the efforts of faith and reason to discern what were some of the processes following upon the initial mystery of creation at the beginnings of things.

✠ John Wright
Bishop of Pittsburgh

CONTENTS

EVOLUTION AND CYCLICISM IN OUR TIME

DARWIN'S VISION AND CHRISTIAN PERSPECTIVES

INTRODUCTION

WALTER J. ONG

Evolution is a term which can still disconcert or hypnotize. For some the concept exists only as a threat, more or less veiled. To others it is the magic password which will open all vistas of reality to the now emancipated mind. To extremists of either of these camps, evolution is a romantic thing, a revolt against the old and an assertion of the new, to which one reacts favorably in accordance with one's predispositions regarding the desirability or undesirability of change.

We need not, however, opt for either of these extremes to be aware of the fact that evolutionary views have deeply penetrated our present thinking in almost every conceivable field. Courses in evolutionary processes and evolutionary theory are now a standard part of the training of biologists and geologists. In pathology, the study of the evolution of viruses and of bacteria as a result of the selectivity imposed by the new antibiotics has become crucial in the fight against disease. We must learn the ways of evolution here in order to control it. In population genetics, the study of evolution becomes charged with mathematics, as tangles of charts and mathematical formulae proliferate in the textbooks with a fecundity which strikes the lay reader as greater than that of the living organisms with which genetics is ultimately concerned.

In virtually all the humanistic fields, it has become regular procedure to study phenomena in terms of their development—which is to say in great part by analogy with organic evolution. Philosophers,

1

economists, sociologists, philologists, geographers, all find themselves making profitable and productive use of evolutionary concepts. The historian, who has a special interest in developmental processes, has enlarged his fields of operation. Where a few generations ago one found chiefly political history, one finds now cultural history, the history of science, the history of ideas generally, of mathematics, of philosophy, of literature, and indeed of any and all fields of human knowledge and activity, including even the history of the writing of history itself. Theologians are deeply concerned with evolutionary processes, not only in interpreting the cosmology of the Pentateuch but also in understanding the development theology itself undergoes as we continue our attempts further to penetrate theologically the revealed mystery of the Incarnation and Christ's continued presence in the world through His Church.

Interest in evolution has moved out of academic circles even into the field of commerce and industry. Here some of the larger and more farsighted organizations have established departments of basic research which devote their energies to development itself, seeking to come upon and exploit new ideas, new insights, and new products which make a rethinking of the organization itself recurrently imperative. For such departments, the subject of development or evolution as such, taken even in its philosophical dimensions, can become a matter of intimate concern. Research workers are encouraged to do things which will keep their minds supple and their thought constantly reaching out for further, often entirely unexpected, insights. The social conditions necessary for development of thought are studied and reflected on.

A recent article, for example, in a chemical-engineering journal advised research chemists to cultivate a close and sympathetic acquaintance with contemporary art. The reason urged was that a mind devoted to basic research needs to see reality in new and fresh and unexpected ways if it is to develop as it should. It needs constant stimulation. The first-rate contemporary artist works sensitively with a feeling for such fresh and unexpected approaches. Because the artist does not work through the laborious process of abstraction, but directly in an artistic medium, he is often well ahead of the scientist in securing fresh, if unarticulated, insights into reality. Although, unfortunately for the scientist, these insights are not scientific ones, they can be of great indirect help. One thinks, of course, of such things as the cubist painters' preoccupation with space which served as an artistic prelude to our present space age, or, further back in history, the development of geometrical vision and perspective in fifteenth century and sixteenth century painters which preceded the great age of Newtonian physics, built on the union of geometry with close visual observation.

What has happened to produce this interest in evolution, in development, in mutational processes which marks our present age? Some, who feel this interest as somehow or other a threat to their security, intellectual or other, may think of it as the result of a "revolt," taking this term, of course, in a depreciatory sense. As a matter of fact, evolutionary thinking is far from a revolt. If its roots are not always readily discernible, they can, as has often been pointed out, in one way or another be traced about as far as one may wish to go in the history of thought. Our new outlook is to some extent a new emphasis.

But it is also more than that. The present interest in development, and more particularly in organic and cosmic evolution, is a product of a central movement within society itself, within the totality of human society around the world. When in the mid-nineteenth century Charles Darwin provided his realistic and penetrating theory of natural selection which changed the idea of evolution from vague speculation to a matter for exact science, he was able to do so because of the way in which mankind had slowly and painfully spread itself over the surface of the earth and was gathering itself together perhaps even more painfully into a total human society.

Darwin's discovery was made possible, and indeed inevitable (in the sense that someone or other would have come upon it soon if Darwin and Wallace had not), by the ease of movement around the surface of the earth and by the relatively rapid communication

which were two of the achievements effectively realized in the nineteenth century. Both biology and geology, the fields in which organic
and cosmic evolution was most fruitfully studied, depend on the
comparison of data which rapid transport and expeditious communication of ideas make feasible. In the case of geology, the need
for comparative study of strata across the face of the globe is
evident enough. Geology is the study of our earth in its entirety,
and hence demands travel and reports on travel. But the full development of biology is equally dependent on travel, if less obviously so.

When they made their famous joint communication concerning
natural selection to the Linnean Society in 1858, Charles Darwin and
Alfred Russel Wallace were both drawing on the results of the com-
parative studies which travel made possible. From 1831 to 1836
Darwin had served as naturalist on the *Beagle*, which sailed to South
America on a scientific expedition. His report on the trip, *Journal of
Researches into the Geology and Natural History of the Various
Countries Visted by H.M.S. Beagle,* published in 1859, has become a
minor classic. Wallace had published his *Travels on the Amazon and
Rio Negro* in 1853, and was actually in the Moluccas when he entered
into communication with Darwin. His account of his 1854–1862
sojourn in the Malay Archipelago was not published until 1869. The
distance separating Darwin in England and Wallace in the Moluccas
at the time of their Linnean Society communication which launched
the concept of natural selection is itself significant. At an earlier date,
when man's occupation of this planet was partial and scattered, such
distances would have rendered the sharing of insights virtually impossible, or at least slowed down this sharing to the extent that intellectual collaboration would be ineffective because too much time
in the collaborators' lives would be lost in discovering and gaining
access to one another. By 1858 such distances had been rather
thoroughly dissolved, and the two men were in effect present to
each other through the media of print and relatively fast written
communication. Their cooperative activity registers a pattern which
is becoming more marked every day as man's intellectual· activity
becomes more and more a matter not only of rapidly shared insights
but also of deliberately planned teamwork.

The principal reasons why travel facilitated and even made inevitable the discovery of evolution are two. First, even travelers who were not trained biologists could not help being struck by the fact that in separate regions the animals and plants were not the same. In the case of the Eastern and Western Hemispheres, even when climatic conditions were the same, the animals and plants were not. What the Europeans knew as the robin and the roebuck had never developed in America, just as the Baltimore oriole and the white-tailed deer had never developed in Europe. Indeed, with relatively few exceptions, every species of animal and plant in one hemisphere was not found in the other. The variations produced by evolution within populations isolated from one another (and now producible under laboratory conditions) were thus spectacularly evident.

But second, travelers who were trained biologists would be struck by a further fact: in many cases—and they soon began to expect in all—two separate but related species inhabiting two geographical regions separate but accessible to each other were found to be connected by representatives in the intervening geographical regions. In these intervening regions, one species modulated gradually into the other, so that there was no one point at which one could say that one species ended and the other began. When one encountered an area, such as a group of islands at sufficient distance from one another, where isolated individuals might on a rare occasion succeed in moving from one region to another with the likelihood that they would thereupon be completely and permanently isolated from the other individuals from whom they had withdrawn, one had an unusually interesting situation for studying variations. Here the blending between species would not be continuous but would exhibit gaps. It was into such an area that Darwin stumbled in the Galápagos Islands, where he made his remarkable studies of the evolution of groups of finches.

The development of communication, including that effected by relatively rapid transport, on which the maturing of geology and biology depended, is not something peripheral to human society. In a certain sense, communication is society. No matter how close individuals may be to one another physically, if no communication takes place between them no society exists. Without communication, human society cannot be, and when society exists its most central and human transactions contain within themselves a germ of communication, of understanding between man and man. The development of communications which has marked the past five centuries, beginning with the dawn of the great age of discovery, and which has more spectacularly marked the generations nearest our own, has been in a way the central productive transaction of mankind. And this development is not ended, as we send our little sputniks and discoverers out into far-off space to beep back to us their reports on how things are out there.

In his early stages man split up into relatively small, isolated units across the face of the earth. For tens of thousands of years, or likely enough for hundreds of thousands of years, mankind was dispersed, lost to itself. Even relatively late in man's history, the most educated ancient Roman or Chinese or medieval or Renaissance man was woefully ignorant concerning even the whereabouts of his fellow men, or indeed concerning their very existence. Most of the surface of the globe—provided that man was aware that the earth was more or less a globe—remained utterly unknown to him, and with it, most of the human race. The part of the race he knew about he knew about almost entirely in the past tense. Current news took weeks and months and years to travel. Even in the area of the globe with which one civilization was familiar, no one could know the actual state of affairs, even in a gross fashion, for the entire area on any given day. A ruler, if he was clever and his couriers reliable and fast, might know how matters stood a month earlier in the north of his empire, two weeks ago in the west, and perhaps six weeks ago in a very remote province.

But today anyone who can watch television or listen to a radio newscast can carry around in his head—and if he is moderately educated and alert, does carry around in his head—a representation of the state of affairs all over the globe. The representation will be far from perfect, in some areas highly defective, and no doubt in some details false. But the over-all effect of the availability of information creates the quite valid sense that in a very real way all men are present to one another simultaneously. Exceptions must be made for retarded regions, but the extent of such regions is daily diminishing. Human society is now actually in possession of the surface of the globe, as it has not been for almost all its existence, and is indeed probing beneath the surface and far out from it into space. With this possession of the surface of the globe, the human race has achieved a new possession of itself through its new technologically devised means of communication, which, for all their obvious limitations, represent an inspiring and utterly central human achievement.

Gaining possession of the globe and of a consciousness of the human race as a real whole has been a long and painful undertaking. The stages in intellectual and technological development which have made our present situation possible are as yet not very adequately understood. But the results have been felt by all, if not with equal keenness. The uneducated as well as the educated are affected by the new sense of simultaneous presence which our communication systems sustain. The uneducated breathe in this sense of simultaneous presence with the radio newscasts which offer them the latest happenings of at least superficial significance across the face of the globe together with the exact hour and temperature every fifteen minutes of their waking lives. They take simultaneity and presence for granted. To the more educated or the more reflective, and particularly to those dealing constantly with ideas, this sense of the presence of humanity to itself is a constant pressure, bearing in on them inexorably all the time, infecting their every thought and movement. They feel themselves as consciously living in new human dimensions to which the writings and wisdom of men who knew only the past afford no direct introduction, but which nonetheless are continuous with and made possible by past experience.

Seen as a product or, if we wish, a paraphenomenon of this unification of humanity across the surface of the globe, the discovery of evolution is nothing strange or new or disturbing, but something with indefinite promise. It represents an improved penetration of reality growing out of a vast accumulation of past experience, taking shape and affecting man at the very center of his intellectual and social being. Evolutionary thinking is thus in a way indigenous to human intellectual activity. It needed only time and experience to mature. Hence it is no surprise that, having come to maturity, it has affected almost every conceivable activity, intellectual and other, in which man engages.

The age in which evolutionary thinking took effective hold of the human sensibility has thus become a kind of intellectual watershed, of paramount importance in our understanding of man's relationship to the reality around him and to God, Who has created a universe far more complex than early man ever imagined. Milton's "well balanced world on hinges hung" has turned out to be more of a "vast profundity" than even Milton could imagine. It is with this thought in mind that the essays in this volume have been brought together.

First conceived of as a group of essays commemorating the centennial of the publication of Darwin's *Origin of Species*, and published in *Thought* during the year 1959, these essays have been gathered here, some in slightly revised form, within the covers of one book. They are by persons with quite diverse immediate interests: a biologist, a philosopher, a theologian, a historian, and a student of literature and the history of ideas. Thus they offer reflections on the meaning of evolution derived from diverse points of view, which, while they do not cover all aspects of evolution and evolutionary thinking, do, in the hope of the authors, treat some significant aspects. All the writers are Catholics, and their reflections, with varying directness or indirectness, seek to understand evolutionary phenomena in terms of even larger perspectives than those of evolution itself, that is, in terms of God's revelation to mankind through His Son Jesus Christ in His Church. The Catholic perspectives are proposed not as restrictive, but as enlarging and liberating, putting the truly marvelous phenomena of evolution into a larger frame of reference where they can acquire still more profound significance.

A HUNDRED YEARS OF DARWINISM IN BIOLOGY

ALEXANDER WOLSKY

In the year 1959 the learned world celebrated the centenary of the publication of Darwin's *Origin of Species*, in which the author explained his theory of evolution by means of natural selection.[1] A few years ago Sir James Gray, professor emeritus of zoology at Darwin's Alma Mater, Cambridge University, reviewing a book on evolution in a rather skeptical vein, predicted that on this anniversary "there may be some heart-searching" and "there will certainly be a great deal of discussion."[2] But there seems to have been more of the

[1] Actually there are two dates to commemorate. The first is July 1, 1858, when the joint paper of Darwin and Wallace was read before the Linnean Society of London under the collective title "On the tendency of species to form varieties; and on the perpetuation of varieties and species by natural means of selection" (published in the *Journal of the Linnean Society*, 3 [Zoology]: 45, 1859). The second is November 24, 1859, when the first edition of the *Origin of Species* was published. The full title of the work is "The origin of species by means of natural selection, or the preservation of favoured races in the struggle for life." During Darwin's life six editions were published, the last in 1872. The numerous re-editions, among them a recent paperback edition (Mentor) with a special Introduction by Sir Julian Huxley, are mostly reprints of the sixth edition. The first edition, which differs considerably from the sixth, has been republished, with interesting remarks by C. D. Darlington, in 1951 by the Philosophical Library, New York. As this article goes into print, the University of Pennsylvania has announced the publication of a variorum text of the *Origin of Species*, compiled by Morse Peckham, showing the many substantial changes which the work had undergone during the six editions in Darwin's lifetime.

[2] "The case for natural selection," *Nature* (London), 173:227 (1954).

latter than of the former. Many of the studies published to commemorate the occasion have turned out to be the customary eulogies,
emphasizing not only the great ingenuity of the author and the
truly epoch-making significance of his theory, but also often con-
veying the impression that the problems of evolution are now largely
solved on the basis which Darwin provided.[3] Although I shall attempt to show that this is not the case and that today, a hundred
years after the publication of the *Origin of Species*, there are still
some controversial points in modern evolutionary biology, it is by
no means my intention to raise a dissonant voice in the choir of
centenary praise for Darwin and Darwinism.

It would indeed be out of line with the tradition of my university,
and of Catholic universities in general, to minimize Darwin's great
contribution to the development of the life sciences. When in 1909
Cambridge University celebrated the centenary of the birth of her
great alumnus, which coincided with the fiftieth anniversary of the
first publication of the *Origin of Species*, the Catholic University of
Louvain sent a special delegate to the celebration, Canon Dorlodot,
a distinguished paleontologist and at that time Chairman of the Department of Paleontology, who read a beautiful eulogy there. Today
a professor of a Catholic university may repeat with equal emphasis
what Louvain's representative said fifty years ago in his address
about Darwin and his work: "Il ne paraît pas exagéré de dire,
qu'en nous montrant la création plus grandiose encore qu'on ne
l'avait soupçonné, Charles Darwin a complété l'oeuvre d'Isaac
Newton; car pour tous ceux qui n'ont pas des oreilles pour ne point
entendre, Darwin fut l'interprète du monde organique, comme
Newton fut la voix des cieux, pour raconter la gloire du Créateur et

[3] A balanced, scholarly memorial volume has recently appeared: "Com-
memoration of the Centennial of the Publication of *The Origin of Species* by
Charles Darwin," *Proc. Am. Philos. Soc.*, 103:159 (1959). (Contributions by
W. E. Le Gros Clark, I. M. Lerner, C. Stern, A. Müntzing, E. Mayr, G. L.
Stebbins, Th. Dobzhansky, N. D. Newell, G. G. Simpson, and P. J. Darlington.)
In process of publication are the contributions to the monumental Darwin Cen-
tenary Symposium held at the University of Chicago in November 1959. These
will appear in several volumes under the title *Evolution After Darwin*, edited by
Sol Tax (Chicago: University of Chicago Press, 1960).

pour proclamer que l'univers est un oeuvre vraiment digne de ses mains." [4]

Darwin's ingenious theory, as he presented it in the *Origin of Species* and elaborated it further in his later works, was indeed one of those great moments in human thinking which, like a flash in the night, suddenly illuminated new vistas for the seekers of truth in the science of life. It gave an explanation, well supported by factual arguments, of how one kind of living beings might have been transformed into, or have given rise to, another type, a process we call today—with a term Darwin never used—evolution. The basic idea of evolution is, of course, not Darwin's invention. The concept that the almost infinite variety of today's animals, plants and microorganisms (estimated conservatively to consist of over two million "good" species) did not always exist in the past history of the earth, but appeared gradually, in succession, and in addition, to some earlier, more primitive forms (or perhaps just one single form of life), as a result of transformations controlled by natural forces—this idea is in fact as old as human thinking. Since the idea of evolution has naturally not only biological but also profound philosophical implications, there were always philosophers with evolutionary views. Among the early Greek philosophers Anaximander and Empedocles were pointed out repeatedly, though somewhat unscientifically, as "evolutionists" having ideas which somewhat resemble Darwin's theory,[5] while in the early Middle Ages the thoughts of St. Augustine on creation sound today surprisingly like the views of some modern geneticists on evolution.[6] In the more recent past evolutionary think-

[4] H. Dorlodot, *Darwinism and Catholic Thought*, Vol. I, The Origin of Species (New York: Benziger Brothers, 1922), Appendix V, pp. 176–177.—Recent appraisals of the Catholic position on Darwinism—apart from the impressive novel views of the great Père Teilhard de Chardin, S.J., but equally positive and affirmative—can be found in the articles of Fr. J. F. Ewing, S.J., "Human Evolution—1956," *Anthropol. Quarterly*, 29:91 (1956), and "Darwinism Today," *America*, 100:709 (1959); see also L. S. Marks, "Darwin 100 Years After," *Fordham Life*, 4:2 (1959).
[5] Cf. Erik Nordenskjöld, *Biologins historia* (Stockholm: Björck and Börjesson, 1925), Vol. I, pp. 13, 23. For a more positive view see the classic work of H. F. Osborn, *From the Greeks to Darwin* (New York: Macmillan Co., 1899).
[6] Cf. A. Wolsky, "Evolutionistische Gedankengänge in der christlichen Phi-

ing played quite an important role before Darwin, not only in philosophy but also in biological sciences, and the ideas of Buffon, Geoffroy St. Hilaire and Lamarck in France, of Darwin's grand-father, Erasmus Darwin, in England, and of the *Naturphilosophen*, including Goethe, in Germany concerning "transformations," are well known. Darwin himself quotes in the Introduction to the later editions of the *Origin* ("An historical sketch") a number of biologists who a few years before him had expressed evolutionary views similar to his, and we know the curious coincidence and convergence of his ideas with those of Wallace.[7]

What then was Darwin's great and lasting contribution to biological progress in general and to the science of evolution in particular? It was a concrete, realistic and penetrating theory to explain how evolution works, what factors transform one type into another. This explanation was so convincing and was supported by such a vast amount of novel observations and reflections that it turned the idea of evolution from a vague speculation into an exact science, the basic tenets of which became axioms for speculative thought in biology. The theory also had an entirely different reception from those given to previous attempts to "prove" and explain evolution (e.g., the theories of Buffon, Geoffroy St. Hilaire, and especially Lamarck), which had left the world of biologists rather cold. From the beginning Darwin's explanation was readily accepted and enthusiastically sup-

---

losophie und in der heutigen Lebenskunde," *Bölcsel. Közlem.* (Proceedings of the St. Thomas Aquinas Soc. of Budapest), 9:18 (1943). (In Hungarian with summary in German.)

[7] A remarkable anticipator of Darwin was "discovered" recently by the distinguished anthropologist L. C. Eiseley, in the person of Edward Blyth, a British naturalist who, twenty-four years before Darwin, developed a biological theory which is in all essential points identical with the theory of natural selection. But, curiously, Blyth used his theory—which, incidentally, was known to Darwin—as an argument in favor of the concept of the constancy of species. Cf. L. C. Eiseley, "Charles Darwin, Edward Blyth and the theory of natural selection," *Proc. Am. Philos. Soc.*, 103:94 (1959). For other anticipators of the principle of natural selection see C. Zirkle, "Natural selection before the 'Origin of Species,'" *Proc. Am. Philos. Soc.*, 84:71 (1941). See also *Forerunners of Darwin 1745-1859*, edited by Bentley Glass, Owsei Temkin and William Strauss (Baltimore: Johns Hopkins Press, 1959) and C. D. Darlington, "The origin of Darwinism," *Scientific American* 200:60 (May 1959).

ported by a large number of his contemporaries. The theory, as the full title of the *Origin* concisely states it, explains evolution in the following way: There is a constant struggle among living beings for food, for shelter, for mating partner and for the other necessities of the continuity of life. In this struggle the forms that fit best into the existing environmental conditions will survive and those which are least fit will perish. The "raw material" of this natural selection is the ever-present "continuous," "fluctuating" variation of the individuals belonging to the same species. The proverbial fact that there are no two leaves exactly alike is another way of saying that variability is a fundamental characteristic of even the purest breed of living beings, and this is the basis of natural selection. From the many slight variants which every species has always in store— individuals of smaller or larger stature, shorter or longer extremities, coarser or finer integumental appendages, and so on—the struggle for life, like a plant breeder or animal fancier, selects and preserves the "good" ones (i.e., which fit well into the existing environmental conditions), while the rest are weeded out. The gradual accumulation of the "good" variants and, of course, the further variation of the offspring in the "good" direction will eventually lead to the establishment of new specific characteristics, differing from those of the original type; and in due time new races, species and even higher taxonomic categories will emerge from the process.

This ingenious theory explained, or at least seemed to explain, in a deceptively simple manner the high degree of adaptation of living beings to their environment and the many instances in which "useful" or "purposeful" organs or functions are encountered. However, it must be remembered that one fundamental point of Darwin's theory —and indeed of all earlier theories of evolution—was purely fictional: the mechanism of heredity. This was a fatal shortcoming. Since individual living beings have a limited life span and, consequently, the long-range biological process, such as evolution, can proceed only through a succession of generations, it is obvious that the success of any attempt to explain evolution will depend on the knowledge (or assumption) concerning the mechanism of heredity:

the way in which the properties of an organism are transmitted to its offspring. But one hundred years ago this was not known. "The laws governing inheritance are for the most part unknown," says Darwin himself in the *Origin*.[8] The general tendency was "to look at the inheritance of every character as the rule, and non-inheritance as an anomaly"—as again Darwin has expressed it.[9] It was also generally assumed that inheritance operates in a constant-intermediary, or "blending" manner. Thus if two individuals were to mate, while differing from each other in a certain characteristic, such as color, or shape, or size of a part or organ, it was assumed that the offspring would show the characteristic in an intermediary degree as if the respective characteristics of the parents were to blend, like two mixing liquids of different color or smell. The offspring showing the intermediary characteristic was supposed to transmit it in this intermediary condition to the next generation, so that hereditary characteristics were constantly "blended," or "diluted" in interbreeding. Darwin's own pangenesis theory of heredity is a good example of what biologists thought a hundred years ago about the operation of heredity. According to this theory all parts of the body give off minute pangenes, or gemmules, which circulate in the body and are absorbed by the cells of the body. The cells thus contain all "information" about the characteristics of the body and eventual changes which affect the body. This is true also of the germ cells, which—when fused in fertilization with another germ cell of the opposite sex —form a new individual with the pangenes of both parental organisms, blended in equal proportion. The individual, of course, transmits its "blend" of pangenes to the next generation—blended further with the pangenes of the other parent. This involves not only a constant intermediary type of inheritance, but also an inheritance of any influence on any part of the parental body during its lifetime prior to germ cell formation, that is to say, an inheritance of acquired characteristics. All this was, of course, utterly wrong but there was no way of knowing it. The day of the Abbot of the Königskloster in faraway Moravia had not yet come.

[8] Chapter I. In the recent Mentor edition the quotation is on page 36.
[9] *Ibid*.

It is therefore understandable that when the true mechanism of heredity was discovered (or rather when it was rediscovered in three instances in 1900) and it turned out to operate in a way entirely different from the assumptions of Darwin and his contemporaries, several points of the original Darwinian theory became untenable. The fact is that hereditary characteristics, or rather their potentialities, are transmitted from parent to offspring not like drops of mixing liquids—nor, for that matter, as blending pangenes—but as independent units which retain their individuality even in cross-breeding and reappear in later generations segregated and unaffected by the company they have kept. The material basis of this behavior, a substance which was localized later with great precision in the nuclei of the cells, is not influenced by the conditions of the body. The substance is firmly encased in oval or elongated corpuscles which appear with surprising regularity at each cell division, are formed from certain components of the nuclei, and are called chromosomes. The chromosomes contain this "stuff of heredity" in a linear, one-dimensional arrangement, similar to a long thread, made up of small segments, each of which is concerned with a different aspect of hereditary characteristics. These segments are conveniently called genes, and it is still useful to describe and interpret the particulate nature of heredity in terms of genes.[10] The genes of the germ cells are extremely constant in their structure and arrangement, and under natural conditions only very rarely undergo sudden, "spontaneous," unpredictable and incalculable changes either in their molecular structure or in their number, or arrangement, which result in changed hereditary properties and which today we call mutations. It is clear that the only source of evolutionary progress is the occurrence of such mutations in the hereditary material of the species and that the existing continuous, "fluctuating" variation is worthless

[10] However, in recent years biologists became increasingly aware that there are a certain overlapping and interplay in the segmentation of the hereditary material; and the concept of the genes as individual and independent hereditary units ("beads on a string"), a concept developed in the second decade of this century by T. H. Morgan and his school, is undergoing today a certain revision; cf. G. Pontecorvo, *Trends in Genetic Analysis* (New York: Columbia Univ. Press, 1958).

from the point of view of evolution because it cannot produce anything really new. The occurrence of mutations was known to Darwin,
too, under other names, but he rejected the idea that they play an
essential role in evolution. His reason for this is quite interesting and
sheds light on another of those weaknesses of his original concept,
which are the consequence of lack of knowledge about the mechanism of heredity. He says: "According to our experience abrupt and
strongly marked variations occur in our domesticated productions
singly and at rather long intervals of time. If such occurred under
nature, they would be liable, as formerly explained, to be lost by
accidental causes of destruction and by subsequent intercrossing." [11]
The last words of this quotation show that Darwin believed in that
conservative role of natural selection upon which he himself did not
elaborate in his works, but which his followers and interpreters, like
Wallace, Romanes, and even Weismann, discussed in detail and
considered rather important. It was supposed to "explain" how
useful characteristics are preserved and sustained in spite of the
alleged "diluting" effect of free interbreeding of "good" and "bad"
variants. According to this concept it is natural selection which pro-
tects the "good" variants from being "washed away," or "watered
down" in free interbreeding. Natural selection prevents this "dilu-
tion" of the advantageous characteristics by eliminating the individuals which carry the disadvantageous counterpart before they
can mate. This preventive and protective-conservative role of natural
selection was a necessary assumption in the days when heredity was
supposed to operate in a "blending" manner. It made natural selection not only the creator, but also the maintainer, the Vishnu as
well as the Brahma of new species.

As a result of this entire erroneous concept of heredity we find
in Darwin's writings everywhere a curious indifference toward the
crucial problem of the inheritance of changes which the individual
acquires during its lifetime under the influence of environment
through excessive use or neglect of certain organs. This was a fundamental assertion of the pre-Darwinian evolutionary theory of La-

[11] Chapter VII. In the recent Mentor edition the quotation is on page 225.

marck, and Darwin did not realize that if it were true (which we know today is not the case) it would be a serious challenge to his own theory. He accepted the inheritance of acquired characteristics as a fact, a logical consequence of his own pangenesis concept, though he maintained that it plays only a minor role in evolution compared with natural selection.

As the various shortcomings of Darwin's original theory gradually came to be recognized by biologists after the dramatic rediscovery of the mechanism of heredity in 1900, there developed a tendency to rescue the valid and valuable elements of the theory, especially the basic idea, the species-creating power of natural selection, and to reconcile them with the "new" concept of heredity, which was soon called, from the name of its originator, Mendelism. For this purpose a sharp distinction had to be made between evolution through natural selection (Darwin's principle) and evolution through direct adaptation to the environment (Lamarck's principle). In other words, the Lamarckian "impurities" had to be eliminated from the Darwinian concept, a task which was undertaken relatively early by August Weismann. Then the whole erroneous concept of the character-diluting effect of free interbreeding and the role of natural selection in preventing it had to be dropped, but this process was completed only after exact calculations were made concerning the consequences of the Mendelian principles of heredity on the composition of natural populations under different conditions, and only after the problem was treated with mathematical methods. Finally, and most important of all, mutations had to be made the basis of natural selection instead of the "continuous" variation. This last change was rendered somewhat easier by the increasing recognition of the existence of so-called micromutations: slight, inconspicuous hereditary variations, which, although appearing abruptly, affect only such "invisible" characteristics as longevity, fertility, resistance to disease, or so-called quantitative characteristics such as size, weight, number of structural elements, and so on. These micromutations come near to Darwin's idea of continuous hereditary variation; consequently, transferring the role of continuous variation to these micromutations made the revision of Darwin's theory seem less drastic than it was in reality.

Mutation and selection together seemed to provide a firm basis for evolutionary thinking, and the new concept, which was based on the knowledge of these two phenomena, became the most powerful factor in the further development of evolutionary biology. This new concept is often called neo-Darwinism, or more recently, and perhaps more correctly, "the synthetic theory" (Simpson, J. S. Huxley), since it is indeed a synthesis, or rather an amalgamation of several concepts, and it is an open question how far it still resembles the original theory, which Darwin proposed a hundred years ago.[12] But the principle of natural selection undoubtedly forms an integral part of it, and therefore the term "neo-Darwinism" or even "Darwinism" is also quite appropriate.

This synthetic theory has found much support among biologists and has achieved, in the last thirty years or so, some really spectacular success, a renaissance of favor which began with the recognition that a realistic approach to problems of evolution can be attempted only on a very low taxonomic level, well within and below the limits of "good" species. It was assumed that the study of the formation of such minor subspecific units, a process which takes place before our eyes and is called—perhaps not quite correctly either from the linguistic or the biological point of view—speciation, will yield results which by analogy can be extended to apply to the formation of new species and higher taxonomic units, processes obviously beyond the reach of human observation. This new approach meant an intensive study of the genetics—and the eventual changes in the genetic constitution—of natural populations, groups of individuals of a species living together under the same conditions and interbreeding freely with one another. The study proceeded along two main lines. One was the fine mathematical analysis of the genetics of populations under varying conditions of mutation and selection by

[12] Dobzhansky, in *Science*, 130:785 (1959), proposes to call it simply "the biological theory."

Sir Ronald Fisher, J. B. S. Haldane, Sewall Wright, and others. The other line was an intensive field work on the phenomena of speciation in natural populations, conducted in the first and foremost place by biologists of Russian nationality or descent, like Tchetverikov, Dobzhansky, Timofeeff-Ressovsky, and by Dubinin among zoologists and Vavilov among botanists. In more recent years, mostly through the magnificent efforts of Dobzhansky, this line of research was linked with cytological studies, and differences in the arrangement of genes—as revealed by the structure of the chromosomes—were found within and between populations of suitable species. Moreover, experiments were conducted in the laboratory with artificial "micro-populations," and the mechanism of evolution became demonstrable almost *ad oculos*. These spectacular results conclusively proved the reality and effectiveness of the evolutionary mechanism as envisaged in the synthetic neo-Darwinian theory, and gave it unprecedented prestige and recognition. This recognition was effectively promoted by a number of excellent treatises on evolution, published in recent years, which have all emphasized the triumph of neo-Darwinism as applied to concrete cases. The works of Cuénot,[13] Dobzhansky,[14] Ford,[15] Huxley,[16] Mayr,[17] Rensch,[18] Simpson,[19] and others in this vein have rendered invaluable service to evolutionary biology by convincing many that the science of evolution is no longer a collection of cloudy theories, but a well-founded branch of biology, based on an impressive array of facts, established with exact,

[13] L. Cuénot (with the collaboration of A. Tétry), *L'évolution biologique* (Paris: Masson & Co., 1951).

[14] Th. Dobzhansky, *Genetics and the Origin of Species,* 3rd ed. (New York: Columbia Univ. Press, 1951).

[15] E. B. Ford, *Mendelism and Evolution* (5th ed.; London: Methuen, 1949).

[16] J. S. Huxley, *Evolution—The Modern Synthesis* (London: Allen & Unwin, 1942).

[17] E. Mayr, *Systematics and the Origin of Species* (New York: Columbia Univ. Press, 1942).

[18] B. Rensch, *Neuere Probleme der Abstammungslehre* (Stuttgart: Ferd. Enke Verlag, 1947).

[19] G. G. Simpson, *The Meaning of Evolution* (New Haven: Yale Univ. Press, 1949).

and in some cases experimental, methods. The effect of these works on biological thinking is well reflected in the universal praise of Darwinism at this centenary of its birth.

The success of the neo-Darwinian trend and its presentation has been so great that we now face a new difficulty of an entirely different nature in contemporary evolutionary thinking: a certain complacent belief that owing to the neo-Darwinian synthesis evolutionary biology has solved its main problems and that all that remains to be done is to work out a few minor details. Of course, this "danger" is a passing one since the history of biology teaches us that whenever periods of complacent stagnation occur, new surprises are not far away, and thus research receives fresh impulses from unexpected quarters. This will probably be the case with evolutionary biology, too, and it is not difficult even today to detect the new lines along which further research will probably proceed. The starting points of these new lines of tomorrow must obviously be the "weak points" of the neo-Darwinism of today.

Such weak points do indeed exist, a fact which is not denied by advocates of neo-Darwinism. One of the most prominent, Theodosius Dobzhansky, wrote not so very long ago of "weaknesses and deficiencies of the neo-Darwinian conception of evolution, which are numerous, as even partisans ought to have the courage to admit." [20] Quite a number of eminent biologists have in the recent past raised their voices against the assumption, made by casual observers rather than by expert specialists, that neo-Darwinism possesses the answers to all the problems of evolution. The objections come especially from those biologists who are interested, directly or indirectly, in problems of ontogeny, the development of the individual from the fertilized egg, since it seems that their findings particularly are at variance with neo-Darwinian ideas.

We may profitably begin a consideration of their objections with the masterly analysis which Richard Goldschmidt, the recently deceased great biologist, gave in his Silliman Lectures at Yale Uni-

[20] Th. Dobzhansky, "Catastrophism versus evolutionism," *Science*, 92:356 (1940).

versity in 1939.[21] In these lectures Goldschmidt pointed out that modern neo-Darwinian research, by concentrating deliberately on evolutionary processes on a very small scale, has necessarily limited the validity of its conclusions to these. The picture of a smooth and steadily progressing evolution by means of natural selection acting on an almost unlimited supply of micromutations may be quite true as long as we are concerned with the origin of minute differences within a species, i.e., the formation of subspecies, races and race groups (*Rassenkreise*) or race chains ("clines"), local ecotypes, and so on. But the crucial question is: Are conclusions concerning the mechanism of evolution drawn from the study of microevolution to be extended to processes of macroevolution, the origin of new species, or genera or even of higher systematic categories? It is a basic assumption of neo-Darwinism that this question must be answered in the affirmative and that there is no essential difference between small- and large-scale evolutionary events. What is true of microevolution must necessarily be true also of macroevolution. But Goldschmidt's answer to the question is an emphatic "No," and he gives a convincing elaboration of his thesis that there is a fundamental difference between micro- and macroevolution. "Microevolution by accumulation of micromutations—we may also say neo-Darwinian evolution—is a process which leads to diversification strictly within the species, usually, if not exclusively, for the sake of adaptation of the species to specific conditions within the area which it is able to occupy. . . . Subspecies are actually, therefore, neither incipient species nor models of the origin of species. They are more or less diversified blind alleys within the species. The decisive step in evolution, the first step toward macroevolution, the step from one species to another requires another evolutionary method than that of sheer accumulation of micromutations."[22] The difference between micro- and macroevolution is also revealed by the lack of true transitory forms between species. Such transitions do exist, of course, on the subspecific level,

[21] See R. Goldschmidt, *The Material Basis of Evolution* (New Haven: Yale Univ. Press, 1940).
[22] *Op. cit.*, p. 183.

but "good species," i.e., distinct taxonomic units, the distinction between which was established by a thorough critical study and where
possible by breeding, are always separated, according to Goldschmidt,
by an "unbridged gap." What is, then, the mechanism of the formation of new species and higher systematic categories? Goldschmidt's
answer to this question is rather unorthodox: the creation of new
types not through slow evolution but through sudden great hereditary
upheavals.[23] To explain this, he contrasts micromutations, which are
considered the basis of evolution in the neo-Darwinian sense, with
the "visible" gross hereditary changes, which occur occasionally in
domesticated, or laboratory-bred animals and plants (the "sports" of
breeders) and change the organism sometimes quite drastically. These
gross and abrupt mutations, which have rendered such invaluable
service in experimental "indoor" genetics, especially in its beginnings,
seem to have little role in evolution, as Darwin had already maintained, although for the wrong reasons. This fact was repeatedly
pointed out since his time.[24] But to Goldschmidt they indicate the
existence, or at least the possibility of other types of hereditary varia-

[23] It should be pointed out here, however, that Goldschmidt's concept is
surprisingly similar to the original mutation theory of De Vries. De Vries was not
only the first to point out that the material basis of evolution is in sudden,
infrequent random changes of the hereditary material, for which he coined
the term "mutation," but he also maintained that these changes usually involve
far-reaching remodelings of the organism, which produce at once new "elementary species." He also expressed the view that mutations occur in certain periods
of the history of life with greater frequency than at other times, and these
periods of mutability are followed by longer eras of no major change. Cf. H.
De Vries *Die Mutationstheorie: Versuche und Beobachtungen über die Entstehung von Arten im Pflanzenreich* (2 volumes; Leipzig: Engelmann, 1901–1903),
and the same author's *Arten und Varietäten und ihre Entstehung durch
Mutation* (Berlin: Bornträger, 1906).

[24] For example, W. Johannsen, "Some remarks about units in heredity,"
Hereditas, 4:133 (1923); R. Goldschmidt, "Das Mutationsproblem," *Sitzungber.
Dtsch. Ges. Vererbg. Z. ind. Abst. u. Verebungslehre*, 30:260 (1923); E. M.
East, "Genetic aspects of certain problems of evolution," *Amer. Naturalist*,
70:143 (1936); A. Wolsky, "Phylogenetische und mutative Augendegeneration
in der Familie der Gammariden," *Magyar Tud. Akademia Ertes.*, 51:645 (1934)
—Hungarian with summary in German; see also *Nature*, 133:876 (1934); A.
Wolsky, "Über einen blinden Höhlengammaride, Niphargus aggtelekiensis
Dudich, mit Bemerkungen über die Rückbildung des Gammaridenauges,"
Verhandl. Internat. Ver. Limnologie, 7:449 (1935).

tion, which differ sharply from micromutations and may be looked upon as more profound changes in the genetic material. He envisages the possibility of a "complete change of the primary pattern or re-action system into a new one" and calls this a systemic mutation. Such systemic mutations, i.e., completely new, entirely "scrambled" or "reshuffled" genetic systems are, according to him, the basis of macroevolution; they are the steps by which new species, and even higher taxonomic categories are formed.

This was a rather startling suggestion, although Goldschmidt tried to bring it into harmony with existing knowledge about the nature of genes. But since in this respect, too, his views were rather unorthodox, and slightly ahead of his time, the majority of biologists, especially the directly interested geneticists, found it somewhat hard to accept the idea of such hypothetical systemic mutations as the basis of major evolutionary steps. However, in the years which have elapsed since Goldschmidt first proposed his new ideas on macroevolution, experi-mental research concerning the nature of the genes and their occa-sional mutation has brought about a number of new discoveries (espe-cially with microorganisms), which have changed quite considerably our earlier views on these matters and have caused a shift in the direction of Goldschmidt's ideas. As Waddington has recently pointed out, the discovery by Lederberg of viral transduction of groups of genes from one bacterium into another and their incor-poration in the hereditary system of the second host (which brought him a Nobel Prize in 1959) has shown that the kind of reshuffling of genetic material envisaged by Goldschmidt is a distinct possibility and therefore one can at least speculate about its mechanism with-out leaving the solid ground of reality.[25] As Waddington puts it, "it seems likely that we are far from having heard the last word about the nature of the variation on which Goldschmidt's unbridgeable gaps depend." [26]

Obviously, the idea of macroevolution by systemic mutations has

[25] C. H. Waddington, *The Strategy of the Genes* (London: Allen & Unwin, 1957).
[26] *Op. cit.*, p. 63.

a number of implications for various branches of biology, but especially in the domain of ontogeny, which Goldschmidt himself has thoroughly explored. (It must be remembered that he was essentially a developmental biologist, and perhaps his greatest contributions were made in the field of developmental genetics, the tracing of the action of genes to early developmental processes.) It is not difficult to realize, and many have pointed this out before Goldschmidt, that any major changes in the hereditary constitution of a germ cell must produce very profound and therefore very early changes in the organism which will develop from that cell. The changes may be manifested as early as the moment of fertilization, or—in the case of the female germ cell, the egg—even earlier, from the beginning of oogenesis. Such changes will therefore affect the mutant's whole development and all the factors that control it. Since these factors are closely interwoven and delicately balanced, any modification, even a slight one, if it occurs in the early phases, will thoroughly upset and remold the "end result," the adult organism, which will be therefore entirely different from its siblings. The mechanism of development can thus explain the occurrence of the occasional giant steps by which macroevolution proceeds.[27] Of course, the drastic changes in early developmental processes will result more often than not in hopeless monstrosities, which will not survive, or will not even complete their development. But those rare instances, in which a change in early development produces a viable new organism, will be the points of origin of new species or even higher types of taxonomic units. As Goldschmidt has epigrammatically put it, macroevolution depends on "hopeful monsters." He also quotes a characteristic paradoxical statement of the paleontologist Schindewolf, who has very similar ideas about evolution: "the first bird hatched from a reptilian egg." [28] This is, of course, not to be taken in a literal sense.

[27] This aspect of evolutionary theory is thoroughly explored also in Sir Gavin De Beer's thoughtful study *Embryos and Ancestors* (Oxford: Clarendon Press, 1951).

[28] O. H. Schindewolf, *Paläontologie, Entwicklungslehre und Genetik: Kritik und Synthese* (Berlin: Gebr. Borntraeger, 1936).

The idea that changes in early ontogenetic processes (produced by systemic mutations) are the basis of macroevolutionary steps has recently found a strong supporter in one of the greatest living embryologists, Albert Dalcq. In several fine essays, one of which is characteristically entitled "Le problème de l'évolution est-il près d'être resolu?" [29] and recently in his brilliant *Introduction to General Embryology* [30] (based on a series of lectures broadcast through the Université Radiophonique of Paris), he explains his embryological ideas about evolution. His conclusion is the same as Goldschmidt's: the major evolutionary steps must have affected "the whole chemistry of oogenesis in such a way as to produce a profound change of morphochoresis" [31] (i.e., visible development). He proposes the term "ontomutation" for the genetic basis of these radical transformations to emphasize their intimate connection with developmental, ontogenetic processes.[32] He thinks that it is "hardly possible" to envisage the major transformations from one egg type of the animal kingdom to another as having taken place by a slow process of trial and error. These major egg types, which he characterizes so masterfully with a few well-chosen words [33] as the egg of the Spiralia "with its specialized cytoplasmic regions and its peculiar pattern of mitosis"; the echinoderm egg "with its double gradient"; the arthropod egg "with its tendency towards postponed cleavage"; the prochordate egg with

[29] In *Annales, Société Royale Zoologique de Belgique*, 82:117 (1951). Other works of Dalcq on the subject include "Le problème de l'évolution à la lumière de l'embryologie causale," *Ann. Soc. Royale Zool. Belg.*, 69:97 (1938); "L'apport de l'embryologie causale au problème d'évolution," *Portug. acta biol.* (Coimbra), Vol. Jub. Goldschmidt: 367 (1949); "Les ontomutations à l'origine des mammifères," *Bull. Soc. Zool. Franc.*, 79:240 (1954); "Brèves réflexions d'un embryologiste sur le problème de l'évolution," *L'Age nouveau*, 105:1 (1959).

[30] A. Dalcq, *Introduction to General Embryology*, trans. by J. Medawar (Oxford: University Press, 1957).

[31] *Op. cit.*, p. 153.

[32] Strictly speaking, the concept of ontomutation is slightly different from that of Goldschmidt's systemic mutation in so far as—in view of the fundamental role of the cytoplasmic architecture of the egg cell in early developmental processes—it envisages a certain influence of cytoplasmic factors in the production of the phenomenon besides the effect of the nuclear (chromosomal) gene system.

[33] The quotations are on page 154 of his *Introduction*.

"polar gradient, cortical field and myogenic cytoplasm"; the amniote egg with "condensed morphochoresis"; and finally the placental egg "with its precocious symmetry and narrow limitation of strictly embryo-forming material," represent respectively fundamentally different organizations and are separated from one another by gaps that are indeed unbridged. The types differ from one another in whole chains of closely geared transformations, which must have arisen simultaneously by one single ontomutation. Dalcq reminds us of the spectacular phenomenon of developmental regulation, which fascinated so many early experimental embryologists: a half egg, or even a quarter of an egg, can produce under certain conditions a whole embryo and indeed a whole viable individual, as even human embryology teaches us in the case of identical (monozygotic) twins. The regulative capacity in present-day eggs may have been the main factor in phylogeny responsible for rendering eggs capable of responding to drastic ontomutations in a constructive regulative manner, and enabling them to produce "hopeful monsters." [34] Dalcq's conclusion is surprisingly similar to Goldschmidt's: "I do . . . believe that there is something more in the evolution of biological systems than mutation and selection." [35]

This similarity of opinion in the case of two great developmental biologists on evolution should certainly make us ponder, even though authority alone cannot be an argument.[36] But the opinions of these

[34] This regulative, "buffering" capacity of developmental processes in relation to both hereditary and environmental changes is the basis of another idea about the role of development in evolution: Waddington's concept of the "canalization of development." It aims at explaining the so-called Baldwin effect, i.e., cases in which recurrent adaptive reactions of subsequent generations to a persistent environmental condition become eventually hereditary and "inheritance of acquired characters" seems to occur. Cf. C. H. Waddington, "Canalization of development and the inheritance of acquired characters," *Nature* (London), 150:563 (1942); *idem*, "Genetic assimilation of an acquired character," *Evolution*, 7:118 (1953).

[35] *Op. cit.*, p. 158. By "mutation" he obviously means micromutations, as distinct from his "ontomutations."

[36] There are other distinguished developmental biologists who have expressed different views concerning the bearing of development on evolution, as for example Sir Gavin De Beer (*op. cit.*) and J. T. Bonner (*The Evolution of Development*, Cambridge: University Press, 1958). For a highly interesting and thoughtful analysis of Darwin's own ideas on the significance of embryology in

biologists are supported also from other quarters. Reference was made already to the views of O. H. Schindewolf, one of today's leading paleontologists, whose convincing advocacy of sudden "outbursts" of macroevolutionary changes in certain relatively brief geological epochs followed by long periods of smooth, "orthogenetic" microevolution, is unfortunately less known in this country than the views of his neo-Darwinist opponents.[37] He points out, for example, that the diverse placental mammals all appear simultaneously in the paleocene and since then hardly any new addition to the group has occurred. Cephalopods had a similar sudden "outburst" in the ordovicium, followed by a long period of relative constancy. The same phenomenon was observed in the successions of stone corals, and several other groups. Such cases, and the conclusions based upon them, certainly deserve attention especially in view of their striking agreement with the evolutionary ideas of biologists who distinguish sharply between micro- and macroevolution, and confine to the former the validity of the neo-Darwinian concept of slow, smooth evolutionary changes.

Even neo-Darwinist biologists feel today the growing necessity of making some distinction, and therefore try to separate micro- from macroevolution, but without accepting the idea of any sharp differences in the mechanism. Thus Dobzhansky suggests [38] that the difference between micro- and macroevolution is that whereas the former is a kind of physiological process, which can be repeated over and over again and can be demonstrated in a laboratory experiment

---

evolution see Jane Oppenheimer, "An embryological enigma in the *Origin of Species*" in *Forerunners of Darwin* (quoted above), pp. 292–322. See also her recent brilliant article "Embryology and evolution: XIX century hopes and XX century realities" *Quart. Rev. Biol.*, 34:271 (1959).

[37] Cf. O. H. Schindewolf, *Paläontologie, Entwicklungslehre und Genetik. Kritik und Synthese* (Berlin: Gebr. Borntraeger, 1936); by the same author, *Grundfragen der Paläontologie. Geologische Zeitmessung, Organische Stammesentwicklung, Biologische Systematik* (Stuttgart: Schweizerbarth Verlag, 1950). Shorter summaries: "Darwinismus oder Typostrophismus?" *Arbeiten Ungar. Biol. Forschungsinst.* (Tihany), 16:104 (1946); "Evolution im Lichte der Paläontologie," *Congr. Geol. Internat.*, C.R. XIX Session (Alger, 1954).

[38] Th. Dobzhansky, "Evolution as a creative process," *Proc. 9th Internat. Congr. Genetics*, 1:435 (1954). (*Caryologia* 6: Suppl.); *idem*, "Evolution at work," *Science*, 127:1091 (1958).

in a "population cage," with predictable results, macroevolution is a
historical process, which consists of unique, unpredictable and nonrepetitive events, changes which occur only once in the lifetime of
the species. But this difference, he maintains, arises simply because
so many mutational and selective possibilities are involved in macroevolution that they cannot all be realized in time, and consequently
the element of chance plays an increasing role in producing the result. The difference between micro- and macroevolution would be
thus merely a difference in the degree of complexity, and one could
even find borderline cases between the two categories in which the
complexity would just begin to appear with an increasing unpre-
dictability and uncertainty of the outcome of laboratory experiments
or field observations with mixed micro-populations, as if there were
just a few too many variables for human beings to control or foresee.
Such transitory cases have actually been labeled mesoevolutionary
by Dobzhansky, and he believes that they prove the absence of any
fundamental difference between micro- and macroevolution.

It is doubtful whether the criterion which he proposes as the basis
of distinction between micro- and macroevolution will be acceptable
to advocates of a more profound difference. What he defines as
microevolution could be perhaps better termed sub-microevolution
(as, for example, seasonal variations in the frequency of certain
hereditary characters in the composition of a population), while his
macroevolution would correspond more or less to what others consider the formation of subspecific taxonomic units, or "speciation,"
i.e., microevolution. In any case, Dobzhansky assures us that in spite
of the identity of the mechanism of micro- and macroevolution there
is a fundamental difference between the two because macroevolution
is creative. This is due to its unpredictable, nonrepetitive character,
which makes it the producer of changes which are new, unique, and
irrevocable, whereas microevolution is more or less stationary, repetitive, and reversible. Dobzhansky quotes Sir Ronald Fisher's statistical definition of the creativeness of natural processes.[39] Natural

[39] R. A. Fisher, *Creative Aspects of Natural Law* (Cambridge: University
Press, 1950).

causation, according to Fisher, can be viewed as the result of a game of chance. "We can imagine ourselves able to foresee all its forms, and state in advance the probability that each will occur. We can no longer imagine ourselves capable of foreseeing just which of them will occur."

Whether one accepts this kind of creativeness as the essential characteristic of macroevolution or prefers to think that the more dramatic creativeness of Goldschmidt's systemic mutations, the production of "hopeful monsters," is involved in the creation of new taxonomic categories of a higher order, the question remains debatable. Goldschmidt's views have often been described as "catastrophism" or even as a "belief in miracles." [40] This is, of course, not to be taken literally, but if we accept the phrase, the difference between the conflicting views on macroevolution boils down to whether one prefers to believe in a few large-scale "miracles" or in a large number of small wonders.

It is not my purpose to judge the tastes, but only to show that there are different tastes, differences of opinion as to the significance of the neo-Darwinian concept in contemporary explanations of the mechanism of evolution. As we have seen, there are serious objections to the view that Darwin's principle of natural selection acting on numerous small hereditary variations (micromutations) has all the answers and provides the only and universal explanation of evolutionary processes, and especially of the origin of higher taxonomic categories.

The existence of such objections to the Darwinian concept should be no surprise to anyone familiar with the history of Darwin's theory in its first hundred years. It is a story of heated debates and controversies from the beginning. Apart from the early opposition to Darwin's views—which were at that time more or less identified with the whole idea of organic evolution and were therefore discussed on a philosophical, ideological level rather than from the standpoint of the specialized scientist—there were biologists from the beginning who objected to it or to some part of it from a purely scientific point

[40] For example, by Th. Dobzhansky in *Science*, 92:358 (1940).

of view. It is well known that even such an ardent early advocate and promoter of Darwin's ideas as T. H. Huxley had his reservations about some details of the theory, and the same is true of August Weismann, who by sharply rejecting the Lamarckian elements in Darwin's theory became the first of the numerous reformers of Darwinism.[41] By making natural selection the sole cause of evolution and proclaiming the *Allmacht der Naturzüchtung* he started a kind of ultra-Darwinist movement, which was soon followed by a period when the theory was sharply criticized and more or less rejected. Neo-Lamarckists, among them the great Oscar Hertwig,[42] started to emphasize—perhaps in reaction to Weismann—the "inner factors" of evolution and the many alleged cases of "direct adaptation" to external influences. Early Mendelian geneticists, like Bateson or Johannsen, attacked the theory from another angle and made natural selection into a negative force. By paraphrasing Weismann's slogan they talked about the *Ohnmacht der Naturzüchtung* in such cases as pure line populations with a near-zero rate of mutations. (There were at that time no reliable data on the frequency of the occurrence of mutations in any species.)

But Darwin's concept has survived this period of declining prestige and, as we have seen, has even made a rather spectacular "comeback" in the last quarter of its century of existence. This is not because the original reasoning became any more convincing, but because there was a constant tendency on the part of Darwin's interpreters to bring his views in harmony with other views and to present compromise solutions, like the synthesis of Darwinism and Mendelism in the early 1930's. The hundredth anniversary finds Darwin's theory in the same situation as the earlier ones: there are still objections to it, even in its greatly revised form, neo-Darwinism, and there are still opposing views which have to be reconciled with it. Today the basic assumption of neo-Darwinism that macroevolution is

[41] There was a time when the term neo-Darwinism was applied to Weismann's ideas on evolution.

[42] Cf. O. Hertwig, *Das Werden der Organismen: Zur Widerlegung von Darwins Zufallstheorie durch das Gesetz in der Entwicklung*, 3rd ed. (Jena: Verlag Gustav Fischer, 1922).

a repetition of microevolutionary processes on a large scale seems to become, with many biologists, a kind of a new *biogenetisches Grundgesetz* (the controversial theory of Haeckel that ontogeny is a brief recapitulation of the evolutionary history of the species and that this phenomenon is the key to the solution of the problems of evolution). But there are unmistakable signs that the opposite view, according to which microevolution is not the whole evolution in a nutshell but only a part of it, is also gaining momentum. There are clear indications that we may expect to see increasing recognition of the necessity for distinguishing between micro- and macroevolution and perhaps even a recognition of the discontinuous character of the latter.[43] How sharp the distinction will be and how far the mode of macroevolution will appear to differ from the neo-Darwinian concept remains to be seen. This question will be probably debated often in the near future, and as heatedly as some years ago the role of the Lamarckian principle, or the role of mutations, was discussed. It seems quite likely that biologists, preoccupied with the analysis of developmental processes, will play a major role in these discussions.

But such discussions, even if critical of some tenets of neo-Darwinism, do not alter essentially its position as a leading concept in contemporary evolutionary thinking. Today the problem is not whether neo-Darwinism is right or wrong, but whether it is the only and the universal explanation of the mechanism of evolution or whether other concepts have to be evolved along with it. In any case, the leading role of Darwin's principle of natural selection in the

---

[43] Cf. R. Goldschmidt, *Theoretical Genetics* (Berkeley & Los Angeles: Univ. of California Press, 1955). In Part 5, pp. 491 ff., he lists geneticists (e.g., Burgeff, Gustafsson, Stubbe, von Wettstein) who have reported recently the occurrence of "macromutations" and seem to be inclined to accept their role in evolution. The latest paper of significance on this subject is Hans Stubbe, "Considerations on the genetical and evolutionary aspects of some mutants of Hordeum, Glycine, Lycopersicon and Antirrhinum," *Cold Springs Harbor Symp. Quant. Biol.*, 24:31 (1959), especially in its paragraph entitled "Evolutionary importance of macromutations" (pages 38–40). Theoreticians of evolution also seem to pay increased attention to macroevolutionary aspects; cf. M. Grene, "Two evolutionary theories," *Brit. J. Philos. Sci.*, 11:110 and 185 (1958); and the same author's "The faith of Darwinism," *Encounter*, Nov., 1959.

formulation of evolutionary theories is now well established and undisputed. And as far as the influence of the Darwinian ideas on biological thinking in general is concerned, even those who are inclined to think that today they form only part of the evolutionary picture must admit that the first hundred years of these ideas represent one of the greatest chapters in the history of biology.

DARWIN'S IMPACT ON PHILOSOPHY

JAMES COLLINS

Darwin's *Origin of Species* records one of man's decisive penetrations in his persistent effort to understand the world and himself. We are different because of its transforming presence, its capacity for unifying the data and theories in biology and for impelling the evolutionary theme into the central position it now occupies in all regions of human thought and sensibility. There are no living sciences, human attitudes, or institutional powers which remain unaffected by the ideas that were catalytically released by Darwin's work and the great efforts at generalization to which it gave impetus, direction, and prestige.

To acknowledge the massive cultural importance of Darwin's own biological findings and of the general evolutionary outlook which it encouraged is not sufficient to dispense us, however, from the usual tasks of careful analysis and critical sifting in the various fields. The human mind is not a mass of seaweed which must simply surrender itself to the prevailing tides: the work of careful discrimination and critical assessment has to continue even at the time when the contemporary mind is keenly aware of how deeply it is permeated by evolutionary ideas. The need for reflection upon the significance of the Darwin centenary is perhaps greatest in philosophy, since it is here that we study the transition from the biological theory of *evolution* to *evolutionism* or the general interpretation of man and the universe in comprehensive evolutionary concepts. This transition is sometimes accomplished insensibly in particular areas of thought where full attention is not paid to questions of method, theory-construction, and the validity of appeals to analogy. But the philosopher's business is to deal with such topics explicitly and to study them in the concrete case of applying biological evolution to all other regions of knowledge and interest. The centenary pause can be made a constructive occasion for renewing the philosophical task of testing the meanings and range of evolutionary speculation in its extended development.

Moreover, the internal growth of philosophy itself during the past hundred years has been strongly shaped by the current of evolutionism. We must continue to agree with the estimate of the *Origin of Species* made over two generations ago by Josiah Royce: "With the one exception of Newton's 'Principia,' no single book of empirical science has ever been of more importance to philosophy than this work of Darwin's." [1] For an understanding of philosophy in its own domestic history during this period, then, we have to examine the various ways in which philosophers responded to the evolutionary theory and sought to give it the function of a universal explanatory principle. Discussions centering upon this issue bring us to the heart of many philosophical achievements and tendencies that determine our present standpoints. The evolutionary premise is none the less real and influential for having attained the privileged status of an accepted framework for contemporary philosophical inquiries.

Here we can only bring into focus a few significant aspects of the philosophical reception of evolutionary ideas. Except for Bergson and some passing references to other men, all of the thinkers with whom we will be concerned belong to the English-speaking world of Darwin himself and his first defenders and opponents. Even within this limit of biologically oriented philosophies, we will have to con-

[1] J. Royce, *The Spirit of Modern Philosophy* (reprint ed., New York: Braziller, 1955), p. 286.

fine the analysis to some points which seem to be historically important and yet which contain some doctrinal significance not yet adequately grasped. The first two sections will consider the drift in Victorian England toward blending a metaphysical agnosticism about ultimate matters with a definite belief in progress on the human scale. In the next two sections, our attention will turn to the spread of evolutionism in America and the specific way in which Bergson made a central issue of the methodology used in every generalized theory of evolution. In the two remaining sections, we will study some representative idealistic ways of treating evolution, as well as the most recent concentration of evolutionary discussion around the thought of Julian Huxley.

1. FROM PHYSICO-THEOLOGY TO AGNOSTICISM

Darwin's story is seldom retold without including a dramatic foreshortening of the whole question of evolution and theistic religion.[2] The famous 1860 encounter at Oxford between Bishop Wilberforce and Darwin's bulldog, Thomas Huxley, resulted in the utter deflation of the former and in the latter's memorable vindication of the seeking and telling of truth in scientific questions. This meeting is often made to do the work of a definitive symbol for an agelong conflict between science and religion, at least a religion having a basis in theism and Christian revelation. When the symbolic transformation of the incident occurs, it then becomes difficult for anyone thinking in these terms to consider it at all likely that theists may still have some good grounds for their assent to God and to man's service of religion. In this common situation, the question of God and evolutionary thought becomes unavoidable. And equally unavoidable is a preliminary historical analysis of the typical views on God which were contested by the early Darwinians. Just as one cannot properly evaluate the customary easy appeal to Kant in ruling out a metaphysics of God without examining the historical circumstances shaping the Kantian

---

[2] See the witty opening chapter of W. Irvine, *Apes, Angels, and Victorians* (New York: McGraw-Hill, 1955).

conception of natural theology, so one cannot effectively deal with the symbolic use of the Wilberforce-Huxley encounter without analyzing the prevalent approach to God which the first generation of Darwinians found inadequate.

The Victorian crisis of unbelief, as induced by evolutionary controversy, has a definite but severely limited significance as far as the underlying philosophical issues are concerned. There can be no question here about an undermining of natural theology as a whole, since the whole range of the philosophy of God does not enter into the actual dispute. There are definite ways of developing a philosophical approach to God which simply do not get explored and weighed by the principal Victorian evolutionists and their theistic counterparts. Newman and his way of individual assent, for instance, stand entirely apart from the two groups actually at odds, and the same can be said about a realistic causal inference from finite sensible being to God. Yet what gives dramatic intellectual importance to the Victorian quarrel is that it does indeed mark the end of the road for one widely accepted route to God: that of physico-theology.

This approach is developed scientifically by Mersenne and Boyle in the seventeenth century, achieves popular form in William Derham's Boylean Lectures of 1711–1712 on *Physico-Theology*, and finds its classical expression as a teaching instrument in William Paley's manual titled *Natural Theology* (1802). There is a fate about these titles themselves. Whereas in his first *Critique*, Kant located the current design argument within a physico-theology, at the outset of the nineteenth century the latter became identified in England simply with natural theology. When Newman at Oxford and Darwin at Cambridge did their required reading in Paley, they were being introduced to all that remained effective at the British universities of the rich variety of ways in natural theology.[3] The latter had contracted itself to what was in effect a physico-theology, and Newman almost alone of his generation was able to make the proper distinc-

[3] G. West, *Charles Darwin: A Portrait* (New Haven: Yale University Press, 1938), p. 78, reports that Darwin knew Paley's *Natural Theology* by heart and admired its logic.

tions and to develop a philosophical approach to God that was not reducible to physico-theology. In large measure, the Victorian crisis over evolution arises out of a failure on the part of men like Darwin, Huxley, and Wilberforce to see that the Derham-Paley position falls pitifully short of encompassing all the resources of the philosophy of God, and hence that it does not deserve to be treated as natural theology without qualification.

Although the Greek and Christian traditions have always appealed to the traces of divine order and providential governance in the visible universe, this general appeal takes its specifically philosophical meaning and cogency from the particular intellectual context within which it functions and by which it is qualified. The novel feature of the Derham-Paley argument from design is that it conforms with the requirements and limitations of modern classical mechanics. The mathematically formulated laws of Galileo and Newton concern the motion and position of macroscopic bodies. But they are not framed to give any understanding of the essential structure of material things, their existential composition and causal dependence in being, or their finality as based upon an act-potency analysis of their principles of being. Physico-theology accepts these restrictions of explanation and hence does not furnish any inferences to God that are based upon the metaphysical considerations which fall outside the scope of Newtonian mechanics. Operating within the phenomenalism and constructural method set by this scientific viewpoint, the appeal to order in the universe takes on a definite hue and shape. It does not deal with the intrinsic finality of agents but confines itself to a study of the design and extrinsic relations exhibited by component parts of the world machine.[4] Within this historical situation, the appeal to cosmic and organic order becomes a design argument and foregoes any metaphysical basis in the study of the finality of finite agents.

---

[4] On this distinction in general, see R. L. Faricy, S.J., "The Establishment of the Basic Principle of the Fifth Way," *The New Scholasticism*, XXXI (1957), 189–208. The critical comments of Hume, Kant, and Mill on the physico-theological argument are examined in J. Collins, *God in Modern Philosophy* (Chicago: Regnery, 1959), pp. 120–21, 164–66, 179–80, 288–92.

The specifying influence of the phenomenalistic and mechanistic context accounts for two special traits of the arguments employed by the physico-theologians. In the first place, great stress is laid upon the analogy of the workman and his product as a way of understanding and accepting the relation of God to the whole universe and especially to the organic sphere. Analogy now takes on a separate career of its own. It is no longer founded upon a direct metaphysical analysis of the need for a causal act to account for composed existents, but instead it becomes an independent basis for leading us to the designer of things. The design argument is based upon a maker-analogy which is liberated from a study of causal dependency in being and hence which seeks to convince us on the strength of the analogy itself. It is because of the analogy of making that we are asked to accept the maker as the actual cause. The only kind of causal activity which God can have within this perspective is of a making sort, and the only ground for requiring this activity is the persuasiveness of the analogy itself. Such an autonomous maker-analogy is particularly vulnerable, since it does not clarify the meaning of causation, the possibility of applying the making activity beyond agents within material nature, and the degree to which an independent comparison can be made between the many, finite cases of making which we do experience and the unique, presumably unconditioned sort of making which belongs to the divine designer. These are precisely the points at which Hume and then Kant attacked physico-theology and forced it to retreat from claims about a design for the entire universe to those for a design of organic things.

Here, however, the second characteristic of the design argument becomes prominent and ultimately undermines the position itself. For this approach to God rests upon showing some deficiencies in the mechanical system, some instances of motion and adaptation which requires the intervention of an intelligent agent over and above the mechanical forces at work in nature. The maker-analogy is to be accepted mainly for the negative reason that we cannot account for certain aspects of the world by means of the scientific principles now at hand. But as both Laplace and John Stuart Mill point out, this kind of reasoning places our acceptance of God upon a temporary basis which disappears as soon as the scientific explanation is sufficiently rounded off to include the facts in question. Without fully realizing what they are doing, the physico-theologians are simply formulating in theistic terms a challenge for science to fill out its own explanation and thus render belief in God otiose or at least founded on some considerations other than the shortcomings of the scientific analysis at some particular phase in its history. This is what Kant means when he says that the "God" of physico-theology is only a limit-idea for scientific explanation, and what the story about Laplace conveys in stating that there is no longer any need for the hypothesis of God in celestial mechanics.

With Paley, physico-theology made one last effort to reach God within a phenomenalistic and mechanistic framework or (as the subtitle of his book phrases it) to furnish "evidences of the existence and attributes of the Deity collected from the appearances of nature." Yet this way of thinking had only maneuvered itself into the negative position of invoking God as a means of filling in the lacunas in the scientific account of the earth and organic adaptations. It could only be expected, then, that the great development of geology in England during the first half of the nineteenth century would also be the story of a constant retreat made by theists, many of whom were themselves prominent geologists.[5] A rearguard action was fought by the defenders of catastrophism, which explained the fossil record by appeal to a series of divine interventions bringing one organic world to a cataclysmic close and replacing it by another. Through the work of Hutton, Cuvier, and above all Sir Charles Lyell, the uniformitarian view finally prevailed, opening up for our minds the vast stretches of geological time and the constant operation of uniform natural forces. It becomes clear that the time-scale used by the

---

[5] For this problem in Great Britain during the background years 1790–1850, read C. C. Gillispie, *Genesis and Geology* (Cambridge, Mass.: Harvard University Press, 1951). "During the seven decades between the birth of modern geology and the publication of *On the Origin of Species*, the difficulty [between science and religion] as reflected in scientific literature appears to be one of religion (in a crude sense) *in* science rather than one of religion *versus* science" (p. ix).

physico-theologians was pitifully inadequate, that species did become extinct, and that constant natural factors could account for
earth strata and their adaptive relations as successfully as for the
formation of the stars.

By the time Darwin was bringing his theory about the origin of
organic species to maturity, the case for physico-theology was also
rapidly shrinking to the region of living things. Here at least, it
seemed quite clear to Paley and his countless readers that divine
agency is needed to account for adaptation in organisms. If any one
balked at being able to trace the connection with a designing mind
as readily in the organism as in the watch, he had a confident reply.
"In the animal, we trace the mechanism to a certain point, and then
we are stopped; either the mechanism becoming too subtile for our
discernment, or something else beside the known laws of mechanism
taking place." [6] But Darwin simply refused to stop at the threshold
of organic nature. He chose to enlarge our knowledge of the range
of mechanism at this point and in doing so he could only conclude
that he was also sapping the resources of physico-theology, which he
identified with natural theology as a whole. In his study of competition and natural selection, chance variation and indefinite divergence
of forms, he felt that he had found the instrument for piercing the
subtlety of the life process by means of mechanical forces, without
appealing to a special creative act for each natural species. The
design in organisms is undeniable as a descriptive fact of adaptive
relations, but the explanation of how it is brought about through
chance variation and other natural factors remains at the level of
the immanent mechanism of nature. There may be a supreme con-
triver of living things, but we are no longer coerced by deficiencies
in biology to say that there must exist such a divine designer.

In his historical situation, Darwin could not avoid viewing every
successful new step in his explanation as being correlated with the
last few steps remaining in the case for God drawn from the appearances in nature. He himself never drove home aggressively the ruin
of physico-theology and only worked out its negative implications

[6] W. Paley, *Natural Theology* (thirteenth ed., London: Faulder, 1811), p. 20.

for his own religious view in a gradual, unemphatic way. He drifted slowly and painlessly from the passive theism of his early days to the *Origin of Species'* concluding remarks on a vaguely supposed super-intending power, and finally to the complete agnosticism and indifference which marked his last years. Darwin's original hold on the theistic conviction had depended on the atmosphere of physico-theology, and as this state of mind gradually faded away before the advances in geology and his own evolutionary biology, it was not replaced by any other living way to God. For him, then, the disappearance of the grounds for Paley's design argument meant the disappearance of all reasonable evidence for the reality of God, and hence his interest simply turned in other directions.

In June of 1860, however, Darwin was still cautious enough about drawing any agnostic implications from his theory of organic evolution to make the following long reply to the religious-minded Lyell, who had warned him against confusing natural selection with the primary creational laws:

One word more upon the Deification of Natural Selection: attributing so much weight to it does not exclude still more general laws, *i.e.* the ordering of the whole universe. I have said that Natural Selection is to the structure of organized beings what the human architect is to a building. The very existence of the human architect shows the existence of more general laws; but no one, in giving credit for a building to the human architect, thinks it necessary to refer to the laws by which man has appeared. No astronomer, in showing how the movements of planets are due to gravity, thinks it necessary to say that the law of gravity was designed that the planets should pursue the courses which they pursue. I cannot believe that there is a bit more interference by the Creator in the construction of each species than in the course of the planets. It is only owing to Paley and Co., I believe, that this more special interference is thought necessary with living bodies. . . . I demur also to your putting Huxley's "force and matter" in the same category with Natural Selection. The latter may, of course, be quite a false view; but surely it is not getting beyond our depth to first causes.[7]

[7] F. Darwin and A. C. Seward, editors, *More Letters of Charles Darwin* (2 vols., London: Murray, 1903), I, 154, 155. Darwin's few guarded statements on religion are gathered in F. Darwin, *The Life and Letters of Charles Darwin* (2 vols., New York: Appleton, 1898), I, 274–86. His preoccupation with Paley

This was an admirable statement of scientific caution in the face of philosophical issues. The only difficulty was that it led only to the negative conception of a noninterfering Deity, for whose causal operation in the universe no positive evidence was being supplied. Darwin was unable to find within the method of biology any reason for admitting some causal activity more basic than the laws of organic evolution and planetary formation. Especially after including man within the scope of evolutionary process, he had no ground in biology for regarding the more general laws as forces imparted to matter by God rather than as immanent patterns of activity without any transcendent reference, as Huxley was suggesting. And Darwin did not acknowledge any method other than the biological one for inquiring into the causal factors involved in the development of man and other living things. In the end, the only sure point was that Paley and Co. had been put out of business by his own explanations and that there were no evident reasons for pushing beyond his account. For the rest, Darwin simply confessed his inability at grasping metaphysical questions and so preserved a calm agnosticism about God.

Our present study of Darwin's gradual repudiation of the design argument suggests that the whole issue deserves some further historical and doctrinal investigation. For one thing, it would seem advisable to reserve the name "the design argument" for that definite sort of appeal to the order in the visible universe which was formu-

---

crops out in his remark that "the old argument from design in Nature, as given by Paley, which formerly seemed to me so conclusive, fails, now that the law of natural selection has been discovered" (*ibid.*, I, 278). He adds that physical evil is more compatible with natural selection than with a providential God, that it once seemed to him unlikely that the whole universe came from blind chance and necessity, but nevertheless that the animal origin of our mind probably incapacitates us for answering these questions with certainty. See M. Mandelbaum, "Darwin's Religious Views," *Journal of the History of Ideas*, 19 (1958), pp. 363–378. The publication of the integral text of the *Autobiography of Charles Darwin*, edited by N. Barlow (New York: Harcourt, Brace, 1958), does not greatly alter the picture of a gradual fading away of Darwin's theism and interest in natural religious belief. But it does make available his critical remarks on Christianity and the account of his relatively early loss of the Christian faith. His interchange of views on religion with other scientists is studied by J. C. Greene, "Darwin and Religion," *Proceedings of the American Philosophical Society*, CIII (1959), 716–25.

lated historically within the framework of modern scientific mechanism and phenomenalism. Moreover, we must discriminate at least five major features in the argument as it was understood by Darwin and his associates, as well as by its defenders among orthodox minds. (1) It is a nonmetaphysical approach to the world and hence does not concern itself with that sort of finality which rests on a metaphysical analysis of action. (2) It is based directly and primarily on the maker-analogy as an independent source, instead of seeking its inferential strength in a causal study as the basis for a causally regulated analogy. (3) As it actually develops, the design argument depends upon the current state of scientific knowledge in the relevant areas. Hence it cannot aim at achieving more than a high probability which always remains open to future revision, in accord with the pattern of scientific research. (4) It sometimes supposes that there is an inverse relation between the limits of scientific knowledge and the extent of theistic assent. Every advance of science would then involve a correlative step of retreat on the part of a design-based theism. (5) Sometimes the proponents of the design argument add that their physico-theology constitutes the whole content of a valid natural theology. It is important to recognize that only the first three traits characterize the design argument in its main historical forms. The last two notes are found specially in the sources studied by Darwin, but they are removable without destroying its import. Unfortunately, Darwin himself does not weigh these various components and consider other theistic ways.

Commenting recently on this whole issue, the anthropologist Loren Eiseley has suggested that "Darwin did not destroy the argument from design. He destroyed only the watchmaker and the watch," that is, he presented a developmental view of nature which simply rendered obsolete Paley's metaphor about nature being a machine with a cosmic machinist as its tinkering maker.[8] But it was psy-

---

[8] L. Eiseley, *Darwin's Century* (New York: Doubleday, 1958), p. 197. R. J. Nogar, O.P., "The Darwin Centennial: A Philosophical Intrusion," *The New Scholasticism*, XXXIII (1959), 411–45, argues that Darwin's theory of evolution inherently denies real intrinsic finality. But his theory is sufficiently complex to bar the flat alternative that he must either accept or reject this finality.

chologically difficult for Darwin and especially for Huxley, who
hardened and universalized the standpoint of evolutionary agnosticism, to slough off the watchmaker approach and still refrain from
concluding that thereby all the empirically ascertainable avenues to
God were cut off for the human mind. Huxley was fond of using
the very terminology of Derham and Paley by referring to natural
selection as a *vera causa*, as a real cause (and in a still more generalized form, as *the* most comprehensive, scientifically knowable
cause), as the precise mode of causal efficiency in which the general
agency of force and matter operates in the organic world. This real
causal interpretation of evolutionary factors gave to time itself a
limitless creative power for bringing about the emergence, modification, and indefinite divergence of all organic species. And when the
causal power of evolution was linked to the universal cosmic forces,
there would seem to be no need for supposing any more primary
sort of causality to which the evolutionary and cosmic agencies themselves would remain subordinate and which would furnish the human
mind with evidential grounds for accepting God's existence.

There were two aspects in Huxley's outlook, however, which considerably weakened this conclusion even for himself. He failed to
examine critically the various meanings for "cause" and to determine
the precise way in which the biological description of evolutionary
process combined causal factors, in the biological sense, with other
types of explanatory reasons. Furthermore, he remained unsure
whether we do or can know anything about matter in its own reality.
And since he conceived of evolutionary forces as the display of matter's causal power in the organic sphere, he could not supply any
ultimate basis for actually ruling out a causal power more primary
than that of the evolutionary factors. Hence there was a curious discrepancy between Huxley's public pronouncements on the ultimacy

---

His thought involves a threefold reference: (1) to the natural world of the
organisms, (2) to the explanatory scheme of his own concepts, and (3) to the
notion of design found in current works on physico-theology. Darwin's remarks
on purpose belong within this threefold context and do not constitute a simple
denial of finality in its metaphysical meaning.

of evolution and his private admission that God may be operating in the universe as the hidden banker or cosmic chess player.[9]

The grand systematizer of evolutionary agnosticism was Herbert Spencer. The very low state of his reputation among present-day philosophers makes it difficult for us to realize the full extent of his influence during the latter half of the nineteenth century or his function as the point of departure for almost all subsequent philosophers of evolution. In his self-revealing essay on "The Filiation of Ideas," he traced the formation of his own developmental outlook to various sources in the pre-1859 period, thus reminding us that evolution was definitely in the air in the decades before Darwin and Alfred Wallace read their famous papers. Spencer acknowledged his debt to Schelling's typically Romantic philosophical view of life surging toward individual peaks, to Lyell's geological work on continuous development of the earth, to K. E. von Baer's embryological study of the trend from homogeneity to heterogeneity, and to some historical studies on the social differentiation and integration of peoples. Darwin only confirmed for Spencer what these earlier sources had already suggested on the evolutionary generalization that all kinds of motion tend from homogeneity to heterogeneity, from the undifferentiated to the differentiated state, and from disaggregation to close integration of parts.

Spencer tells us that the habit of selecting evidence for its value as illustrating this evolutionary pattern was strengthened in his mind by the need for some general conception to replace the outworn theory of special creation of the various forms of nonliving and living things.

In 1852 the belief in organic evolution had taken deep root, and had drawn to itself a large amount of evidence—evidence not derived from

[9] Huxley's private waverings come out most clearly in correspondence with Charles Kingsley and are examined in Irvine, *Apes, Angels, and Victorians*, pp. 127–34. William Irvine has also described the turmoil aroused in Tennyson, Hardy, and other poets by evolutionary views of nature: "The Influence of Darwin on Literature," *Proceedings of the American Philosophical Society*, CIII (1959), 616–28.

numerous special instances but derived from the general aspects of organic nature, and from the necessity of accepting the hypothesis of Evolution when the hypothesis of Special Creation has been rejected. . . . From this time onwards the evolutionary interpretation of things in general became habitual.[10]

It is noteworthy, however, that Spencer's rejection of the Derham-Paley position does not lead him to atheistic naturalism or to the thesis about the warfare of science and religion. Quite to the contrary, he concludes that science and religion can now be reconciled on the ground of their common recognition of the unknowable. They both admit that there is an absolute which transcends our ability to know or conceive, beyond the bare affirmation of its presence.

Underlying this interpretation is Spencer's own philosophical phenomenalism, which is more radical than that of Hamilton and Mill. Neither through scientific nor religious means can the human mind advance its range of knowledge beyond the sensible phenomena and their immanent laws. We can indeed ascertain the laws of order according to which the changes in the cosmos occur, but such a descriptive pattern "still leaves unexplained the *nature* and *origin* of them." [11] It is enough to know that phenomenal events and their immanent laws do have a nature and origin in order to conclude to the reality of the absolute, but we cannot advance a single step beyond this affirmation. All we can try to do is to apply to the unknowable our own subjective and symbolic conception of cause or power. But neither the scientist nor the religious mind can transcend the symbolic mode of signifying the unknowable absolute, and precisely in

[10] D. Duncan, *Life and Letters of Herbert Spencer* (2 vols., New York: Appleton, 1908), II, 319. (The text is from Spencer himself, who wrote about his own development in an impersonal mode.) For scholarly research on the pre-Darwinian history of evolutionary theories, H. F. Osborn's *From the Greeks to Darwin* (revised, second ed., New York: Scribner, 1929) has long been outmoded by the work of Lovejoy, Zirkle, and others; Eiseley gives a good description of the two generations of scientific thought before Darwin in *Darwin's Century*; a new reading of the sources is made by W. Zimmermann, *Evolution: Die Geschichte ihrer Probleme und Erkenntnisse* (Freiburg and Munich: Verlag Karl Alber, 1953). But the best report of recent findings is the collection of essays by B. Glass and others: *Forerunners of Darwin, 1745–1859* (Baltimore: Johns Hopkins Press, 1959).

[11] In Duncan, *Life and Letters of Herbert Spencer*, II, 334.

this joint disability to specify it any further lies the principle of their harmony. Thus Spencer regards an evolutionary agnosticism as the best means of reconciling science and religion in our age.

What still keeps Spencer's position intriguing is the way it combines agnosticism about the nature of the material world and God with a resolute systematizing of the human sciences and realms of experience. Within the phenomenal order, he is unlimitedly hopeful about the synthetic power of his evolutionary formula. It becomes a synthetic principle by moving beyond the biological procedures of assembling empirical facts, proposing inductive hypotheses, and supplying particular verifications for them. Evolution as a philosophy and not simply as a theory in biology or any other special scientific field depends upon the rule of giving a *deductive* interpretation to all inductively established positions.[12] Philosophical evolutionism rests upon this conversion of factual inductions and their attendant theories into necessary deductive consequences of the most universal phenomenal principles. Until this deduction is made, Darwinian evolutionary thought is regarded by Spencer as infraphilosophical.

Even the particular laws of evolution must be shown to be deductively related to the laws of motion and the supreme principle of the persistence of force. Spencer observes that the latter is not properly called the "conservation of force," since this might lead to illusory inferences to a conserver or some conserving act that would violate the phenomenal limits of human knowledge. The persistence of force is indeed the first deductive principle of the evolutionary system, but no ontological inferences can be drawn from it. In respect to the absolute, it is only the scientific way of making a symbolic reference to the unknowable something as being the powerful core of the universe.

Spencer was quite abstemious in his use of factual studies, being content with using a minimal amount of materials for suggesting an evolutionary pattern for some special area. His synthetic philosophical principles for biology, psychology, and sociology sought mainly

---

[12] *Ibid.*, II, 313–14, 323, 326 (against Huxley); Herbert Spencer, *First Principles* (sixth ed., Akron, Ohio: Werner, 1900), p. 502.

to introduce a deductive rigor into these sciences by showing their necessary connection with his more general statement of the persistence of force, the laws of motion, and the formula for evolution. He made a peppery defense of this deductive procedure against Huxley by noting that biology and other sciences do not achieve their full standing within philosophical evolutionism until the deductive entailment is established. At the same time, he rendered his entire synthetic enterprise highly vulnerable to any attack concentrating on the concept of force. This was precisely the point singled out by Henri Bergson in his Collège de France lectures for 1904–05:

If one attributes here to the word "force" the meaning which the scientist gives to the word "energy," Spencer's conclusions must be greatly restricted. If, on the other hand, one takes the word in the broader meaning in which Spencer often seems to use it, the conclusions of this philosophy lose the basis which he thought to find for them in positive science.[13]

Bergson was suggesting that Spencer either had to sacrifice his grandiose systematic deduction of all areas of knowledge or else admit that it is lacking in scientific rigor. Taken in conjunction with the twentieth-century developments in the concept of energy, this criticism contributed toward the rapid erosion of Spencer's version of evolutionary agnosticism.

2. EVOLUTION AND PROGRESS

There is another aspect of Spencer's philosophy which is still worth examining: its quite ambiguous support of the theory of continuous progress. All that his evolutionism can strictly guarantee from its deductive basis is the persistence of force, which means the persistence of relations among forces, together with the transformation and equivalence of forces in a Newtonian system. This accounts for the highly qualified manner in which he describes the evolutionary formula: "The re-distribution of the matter and of its retained mo-

[13] H. Bergson, Écrits et paroles, tome I (Paris: Presses Universitaires, 1957), p. 234.

tion, is from a relatively diffused, uniform, and indeterminate arrangement, to a relatively concentrated, multiform, and determinate arrangement." [14] The evolutionary trend is a relative one, because it is limited in principle by the equally basic movement of dissolution. The play of forces is a constant making and unmaking of the material order, with a probable tendency toward a total equilibrium of forces. As to whether we can state categorically that the cosmic process must terminate in a total extinction of all changes, Spencer maintains that this question concerns something ultimate and hence belongs in the realm of the unknowable. A universal quiescence is a possible outcome but we cannot show it to be inescapably necessary. There is also an open possibility of indefinitely continuing the cycle of renewal and destruction, integration and disintegration, concentration and dispersion.

Spencer assures us that he himself leans toward the latter alternative. But he does so only as a matter of belief and reasonable inductive inference from organic and human development. The difficulty is that the hope for an indefinite alteration cannot be justified through any deductive argument from the persistence of force. According to Spencer's own methodology, therefore, his belief cannot acquire the standing of philosophical knowledge and cannot be regarded as a necessary consequence of evolutionism. There must be an element of strong natural faith behind any theory of progress which appeals to the evolutionary philosophy of Spencer for support.

Even if we do accept this view, however, the aid it gives to progress is only relative and temporary. Strictly speaking, what remains possible within the context of the Spencerian persistence of force is not evolution alone but the conjunct law of evolution-and-dissolution, the indefinite alteration of the processes of forming and dissolving. As a demurrer against the necessity of a universal heat-death, evo-

[14] *First Principles*, p. 501; cf. pp. 484, 492–93, 505–06. S. F. Mason, "The Idea of Progress and Theories of Evolution in Science," in *Essays on the Social History of Science*, edited by S. Lilley (Copenhagen: Munksgaard, 1953), pp. 90–106, shows that evolutionary thought has given rise to various theories of progress, but he does not stress the anti-progress and cyclic inferences that have also been made from it.

lutionary agnosticism can only offer the possibility of an everlasting cycle of making and unmaking of all the structures involved in human experience of the world.

This is the point which Friedrich Nietzsche seeks to drive home with the hammer blows of his doctrine on the eternal return of the same state of affairs.[15] He contends that Spencer is too timid to acknowledge that cyclic alteration is not just a likelihood but the essential law of the universe. And Nietzsche suggests that the reason for the hesitation is found in the social and historical consequences of a thoroughgoing cyclism. Once we have tasted the Judaeo-Christian hope for an open-ended conception of time and history, we are reluctant to embrace the full consequences of evolutionism-and-dissolutionism and cannot summon the courage to engage in human affairs within this framework. For Nietzsche, the superman is by definition the mind which can lucidly accept the graven law of a cyclic return of everything to the same point and nevertheless work energetically within the present span of time.

Spencer and the so-called Social Darwinists in England and America might reply to Nietzsche that he has overstepped the limits of phenomenalism in treating cyclism as an essential law of ultimate reality. But even within their own context, they would have to concede that Spencer's favorite slogan about the survival of the fittest provides no strict guarantee of the endless improvement of the stock and especially of human society through competition. From the philosophical standpoint, evolutionary social meliorism has to be qualified by the distinction between a short-range and a long-range estimate. Within the brief era of modern science and industry, Spencer can point out that the prevailing trend is a gradualist evolution and slow spread of organized altruism. But he admits that this era belongs within an enormously broader time scale and is likely to lead to a dissolutional phase of human history. Taking this cosmic per-

[15] On Nietzsche's ambivalence toward Darwinism, cf. W. Kaufmann, *Nietzsche* (Princeton: Princeton University Press, 1950), pp. 126–27, 288–89. Nietzsche approved of its stress on universal change and man's animal origin, but he criticized it for not seeing that only a few choice spirits rise above the species level and for not facing up to eternal recurrence.

spective, he finds it difficult to avoid the conclusion that social progress will inevitably be undone and the achievements of cultural integration dissolved. His social drive works in favor of short-range
improvement but his synthetic principles do not yield any philosophical confirmation of the faith in long-range progress.

More recent evolutionary thought usually regards the developmental process as being unique and irreversible, although not always
as progressive. This is often due to a resonance of Christian faith or
of a natural faith in the significance of human history.[16] Another
factor is the refusal of many biologists, anthropologists, sociologists,
and interpreters of history to follow Spencer in seeking a deductive
philosophical justification of their position. Thus they can avoid his
quandary about whether or not to treat the irreversible and progressive view of time as a consoling parochialism holding good only
within a limited reach in the biological and historical spans of time.
Yet the consequence is that they do not share in Spencer's clarity
about the noetic status of what he called the belief in progress as a
beneficent necessity of the evolving cosmos. The contribution of
Christian faith and of philosophically determinable evidence to this
conviction has to be carefully weighed, if illusory interpretations of
progress are to be discovered and eliminated.

As expressed in *The Descent of Man*, there are some unsettling
features in Darwin's own theory which prevent any easy acceptance
of automatic, universal progress.[17] In so far as he accepts the uniformitarian (rather than the catastrophic) reading of the geological
record, he is anticyclical and supports an open movement toward ever
new forms of life. But he also criticizes a simplistic kind of progres-

---

[16] The influence of natural and revealed faith is studied by J. Baillie, *The Belief in Progress* (New York: Scribner, 1951).

[17] Relevant sections from *The Descent of Man* are conveniently presented in the source readings edited by F. J. Teggart with introduction by G. H. Hilde-brand, *The Idea of Progress* (revised ed., Berkeley and Los Angeles: University of California Press, 1949), pp. 448–53. The theme of J. C. Greene's *The Death of Adam* (Ames, Iowa: The Iowa State University Press, 1959) is that scientists applied evolutionary ideas only gradually and reluctantly to man, and that Darwin's own view of man remained basically ambiguous about the moral quality of man's future developments.

sionism which arranges all the forms of life in a single ladder of nature pointing climactically to man's perfection as the highest rung. The image of the ladder of nature does not necessarily involve a relation of descent among the arranged forms, whereas Darwin insists on the genetic descent of related organisms. Furthermore, his stress on the indefinite divergence of species demands a new metaphor, that of the continually branching tree of life, instead of the serial set of rungs along a single track.

These modifications have one further implication: Darwinism cannot enter into a simple alliance with the philosophical forms of the theory of progress popular during the eighteenth and nineteenth centuries. Both the physico-theologians and the Encyclopedists accept progress in the sense of a convergence of everything toward man and an indefinite perfectibility of man himself. For the Darwinian mind, however, man is one apex among many in nature, and he is an apex which is the genetic outcome of a development from simpler organisms. The latter do not merely point toward man and subserve his needs: they give rise to the human organism along one of the lines of descent, without depreciating other lines and other peaks. The biological evidence alone does not furnish distinctive grounds for constant improvement to be the law of man's history. Other sources of evidence about man must also be consulted, and then there is the task of evaluating several reports and not simply of construing the idea of progress as the massive and inevitable conclusion of scientific studies.

The plural lines of descent also make it difficult to integrate the biological with the current philosophical meanings of development. When the Romantic mind or the Hegelian dialectician or the Comtean positivist declares that nature is undergoing development, he implies that this process is tightly organized according to rational laws and that it is ultimately unified in a convergent development toward man. But the Darwinian evolutionists specify that the evolutionary mechanism depends on chance variation, natural selection, and indefinite divergence of species. This view of the precise means of biological development need not be incompatible with every sort of belief in progress, but it does not specifically furnish confirmatory evidence for the reign of rationality and the convergence toward man's welfare upon which the prevailing philosophical conceptions of progress rested. The biological meaning for development cannot simply be equated with the philosophical sense elaborated by idealism and positivism, and hence a theory of man-centered progress is not an unavoidable corollary of biological evolution. The Social Darwinists clouded over this issue temporarily, but it was bound to reassert itself under less favorable social conditions and in a reflective analysis of the logic of Darwinian evolution.

Darwin himself concluded the *Origin of Species* with the hopeful picture of an indefinite progress on the part of all biological species, since they are not fixed in their present limits. But his recognition of the play of chance in nature and the interplay of complex nondirectional factors in the environment prevented him from giving unhesitant assent to progress as the intrinsic law of organisms and especially of human social life. In *The Descent of Man*, he did regard the progressive viewpoint as truer and more cheerful than that which centers on an original perfect state from which we have fallen, but he was aware of too many variable elements in human life to treat natural selection as a rigid law operating for social progress. The evolutionary tendency toward integration, complexity, and differentiation could not be interpreted as a constant improvement, unless one identified such trends with the evolutionary phase in Spencer's cycle of change. Then, however, one would also have to admit that the downward trend of cosmic force would eventually prevail over temporary advances of man and other organisms in a counterdirection. This was the point of Huxley's disenchanting remark, in his notable Romanes Lecture on evolution and ethics, that "the theory of evolution encourages no millennial anticipations." [18]

[18] "Evolution and Ethics," reprinted in the joint volume by T. H. Huxley and Julian Huxley, *Touchstone for Ethics* (New York: Harper, 1947), p. 93. Even the positivist historian, J. B. Bury, was so impressed by Thomas Huxley's view that he admitted that evolutionary theory remains neutral and "lends itself to a pessimistic as well as to an optimistic interpretation."—*The Idea of Progress* (reprint ed., New York: Dover, 1955), p. 345.

Rather, it was at the nonmillennial level or within the limited perspective of cultural history that there was some hope of forestalling for a while the completion of the full cosmic cycle of unmaking what natural selection and human art have made. Hence Huxley spelled out the condition under which evolutionary theory could be joined with a belief in progress: only if a temporary dualism were maintained between the state of nature in its plenary scope and the restricted order of human art. This involved a philosophical consideration and a decision which could not justify themselves on the ground of being only a sheer extension of the findings of biological evolution.

The thorough ambivalence of the relation between biological evolution and belief in progress explains why the sharp decline of the latter in the twentieth century has not undermined evolutionary thought among biologists. The crisis in theories of progress brings out the need for distinguishing clearly between biological development and the philosophical meanings for development in nature and society. And if there is indeed a millennial aspect to the acceptance of progress, its roots are to be sought partly in the Christian faith and its providential conception of all cosmic change and human history.[19] The act of accepting some sort of progress in time and human history is never a simple and univocal act, having the same meaning for all minds. The theme of progress is a complex locus today where scientific, philosophical, and religious elements are conjoined in many different ways by the individual mind. At least, a study of the nineteenth-century biological evolutionists shows that the coming of Darwinism did not relieve anyone of the responsibility to sift these various factors critically before making one's personal evaluation of the problem.

3. EVOLUTIONARY PHILOSOPHY IN AMERICA

The relation of evolutionary thought to physico-theology, agnosticism, and the theory of progress was primarily the story of its effect

[19] For the Christian and naturalistic background of modern millennialism, consult E. L. Tuveson, *Millennium and Utopia* (Berkeley and Los Angeles: University of California Press, 1949).

upon philosophies already in being. In migrating to America, however, it played a germinal role in forming and directing some new scientifically oriented philosophies. During the speculative doldrums of the decade 1850–60, it would have required a hardy prophet to say that America was on the threshold of a philosophical renaissance which would control the course of thought for the next century. That this quickening did actually occur was due in large measure to the discussions aroused by the introduction of Darwin and Spencer to our soil. Their stimulus upon the philosophical minds maturing from 1860 to 1890 was a major contribution to the development of pragmatism in its several varieties.

Our concern is not with the American Social Darwinists and their apology for competitive individualism, since these men were singularly barren in new ideas and methods for philosophy.[20] But amid the gusts of economic and social propaganda, a few men were engaged quietly in examining the basis of evolution and its implications for philosophy. During the 1860's and 1870's a group of Harvard men, including Wright and Green, Peirce and James, Fiske and Holmes, met informally to discuss philosophical issues. Peirce liked to call them members of his Metaphysical Club, and in any case they were the seminal source of the pragmatic current of thought in America.[21] One of their major topics was evolution and the effect it would have upon the philosophical conception of man and knowl-

[20] R. Hofstadter, *Social Darwinism in American Thought* (revised ed., Boston: Beacon Press, 1955), discusses the vogue of Spencer, the ethical influence of Huxley, and the reaction of James and Dewey. A broader account of evolutionary ideas in America is provided in the essays edited by S. Persons, *Evolutionary Thought in America* (New Haven: Yale University Press, 1950), especially the chapters on the rise of evolutionism and its effect on ethics and theology.

[21] The best study of this group is P. P. Wiener's *Evolution and the Founders of Pragmatism* (Cambridge, Mass.: Harvard University Press, 1949). Also informative are the briefer accounts by H. W. Schneider, *A History of American Philosophy* (New York: Columbia University Press, 1946), pp. 321–437, and by M. H. Fisch, "Evolution in American Philosophy," *The Philosophical Review*, LVI (1947), 357–73. The two latter authors stress the application of evolutionary ideas to man, whereas the viewpoint of the present study is directed toward the underlying problems in methodology and causality which remain lively issues today. For the rearguard action of the older Scottish school, see J. McCosh, *The Religious Aspect of Evolution* (revised ed., New York: Scribner, 1890).

edge and the universe. Historically considered, their approach to this nest of questions was unique in that they probed more fundamentally and critically into the philosophical meaning of evolution than did any other contemporary minds. And it can be added that the problematic character of evolutionism as a philosophical postulate was more vividly realized and objectively probed by these men than by their successors, many of whom tend to accord to it a dogmatic status which this pioneer group would scarcely countenance.

For our purposes, the key individuals are Chauncey Wright and Charles Peirce. Wright was affectionately called the boxing-master of the group, since they all had to face the challenge of his bold analyses and his project of assessing Darwin and Spencer in the light of Mill's logic of the sciences. His contribution lay precisely in the resolve not to play favorites with evolutionary speculation but to submit it to the ordinary canons of scientific method. Whereas Spencer, Haeckel, and lesser popularizers had uncritically used Darwin's theory to advance their own sprawling cosmological views, Wright recommended a reflective methodological study of evolutionary theory to determine its proper scope and its relation to philosophical topics. In carrying out this program, he made a devastating criticism of Spencer and succeeded in detaching the Harvard group from the synthetic philosophy long before it reached completion and full popular acceptance.

There are four main points in Wright's critical analysis of Spencer: the nature of principles, the meaning of force, the inductive use of examples, and the relation of scientific method and metaphysics.[22] (1) Spencer plunges directly into the work of grinding out philosophical principles for the several sciences, without stopping to inquire whether evolution or any other principle can have the same meaning in science and in philosophy. The working scientist regards a principle as an eye for looking beyond itself at some regularities discoverable among concrete events, but he does not regard a prin-

[22] His core ideas on science and evolution are available in *The Philosophical Writings of Chauncey Wright*, edited by E. H. Madden (New York: Liberal Arts Press, 1958), pp. 12–42. On Darwinism and earlier philosophies of science, consult A. Ellegard, "The Darwinian Theory and Nineteenth-Century Philosophies of Science," *Journal of the History of Ideas*, XVIII (1957), 362–93.

ciple as an active component in the events themselves. From this standpoint, Spencer and other uncritical evolutionists mistake the tool for the handiwork. They disclaim metaphysics and yet they make their evolutionary principles function as constitutive causal agencies in natural process itself. Wright advises us to restrict the evolutionary principle to its explanatory role, without claiming any real causal significance for it, at least when we treat the principle as a scientific one.

Another trait of a scientific principle is its definite and revisable relation to what we can experience. Granted that it enjoys some relative stability and universality, still as a working scientific tool it never completely divests itself of its role as a leading question, as a scaffolding which will eventually give way after serving in some definite capacity. But Spencer treats the persistence of force and evolution as completely definitive, nonhypothetical principles whose deductive range reaches to the entire universe. His justification is that these principles express in abstract and generalized form the ultimate phenomenal truths about the process of things. Yet this supposes that a definitive understanding has already been reached in the major sciences and hence that the only further need today is for principles which are summarizers of a complete and universal truth. Even within the framework of classical physics, however, Wright can point out that there are areas for fundamental research and hence principles in the more typically scientific sense of interrogators of nature or investigative leads for uncovering new aspects of nature.

Spencer never establishes in detail the transition from principles in this latter sense to his own philosophical notion of principles as abstract summarizers of a fixed totality of knowledge. In the scientific context, the evolutionary principle does not cease to be open to revision and deep modification of its import, regardless of the philosophical mansions built upon its meaning at some given stage of biological research. Wright does not dispute the need for abstract and broadly formulated principles in science, but he does insist that their purpose is rather to open our minds to new problems and observations of concrete events than to serve as deductive premises for a set of incorrigible truths about all events and relations in the cosmos.

(2) Spencer defends his distinctive philosophical use of the evolutionary principle on the ground that it is strictly deducible from the persistence of force. His further remark that "persistence" is preferable to "conservation," since the latter signifies a causal substrate or ultimate conserving source, rouses Wright's suspicion. Either Spencer does not grasp the Newtonian physical-system meaning for force or else he is using physical terms in an equivocal way in order to profit by the prestige of physics, but without assuming any of its methodological limitations. Anticipating Bergson's line of attack, Wright notes that in all his multivolumed enterprise Spencer fails to supply any extended account of physics itself, so that we may follow the steps in transforming the physical concepts of force, energy, and conservation into the deductive basis of the synthetic philosophy. Instead, he fuses many different meanings for "force" into a nebulous concept whose scientific grounding cannot be tested in any specific way.

To all the ideas which he [Spencer] adopts from science he adds a new sense, or rather a vagueness, so as to make them descriptive of as much as possible. . . . Out of mathematical formulas these terms lose their definiteness and their utility. They become corrupting and misleading ideas. They are none the less abstract, but they are less clear.[23]

The subsequent preoccupation of the pragmatists with finding ways of making our ideas functionally clear stems partly from a resolve to avoid such irremediable cloudiness. Wright's immediate conclusion here is that the first principle from which Spencer deduces his evolutionary law is hopelessly vague and hence cannot supply any scientific warrant for converting the biological notion of evolution into a full-blown philosophical evolutionism.

Spencer's law of evolution may be a consistent necessary consequence of his own notion of force, but there is no way to trace a scientific ancestry for the latter. Wright suggests that it may be an original expression of Spencer's subjective interests and aspirations toward system-building, but then its import is emotive and not scien-

---

[23] *The Philosophical Writings*, pp. 24, 25.

tific. Once the principles of evolution and persistence of force are wrenched from a definite context of predictive hypotheses, experimental situations, and mathematical formulas, they enter the realm of scientific unknowables. We should therefore be just as prudently agnostic about them in their philosophical use as Spencer is about the nature of the unknowable absolute.

(3) A defense of Spencer might be made by appealing to his inductive procedure of citing examples of evolution from many sciences. In reply, Wright notes that, with the exception of a careful report of von Baer's work in embryology, his examples are loose restatements ranging from the nebular theory to the history of Roman laws. Spencer has a penchant for concentrating his inductive materials in such areas as the formation of the stars and the transition from the inorganic to the organic, areas where our present knowledge is most problematic and open to further revision. Furthermore, there is a decisive difference between the scientific effort of *universalizing* a position through deductive prediction and empirical verification and the Spencerian method of *generalizing* scientific data by means of noting loose similarities and then capping them into a law for the cosmos. The evolutionary law is the result of such a generalizing process. The references to increasing heterogeneity and integration evoke many analogies, but they do not permit of any determinate testing for validity. In this respect the philosophical use of evolutionary analogies is just as loose as the watchmaker analogy of the physico-theologians.

Once more, then, Wright returns to the question of the source of the philosophical idea of evolutionary change. He grants that this idea exerts a powerful influence upon the contemporary mind and serves an effective unifying function. But in this highly generalized and analogical form, its source is to be found in the human mind's inclinations and dreams rather than in biological research. It is the outcome of transforming the limited Enlightenment belief in social progress into a universal belief in the progress of the whole universe. Using Mill's distinction between what we know by inductive belief and what we hope for through imagination, Wright assigns philosophical evolutionism to the latter point of origin. He attributes the powerful belief in evolutionism to the operation of "the moral and mythic instincts," to our human need for some kind of moral faith and mythopoeic imagery with which to interpret the universal fact of process in the world.[24] This does not necessarily mean that the evolutionary outlook is illusory but only that it is something other than a continuous expansion of the biological theory of evolution or a rigid deduction from some wider physical principle. The philosophical principle of evolution is not founded on the natural sciences but reflects the moral hope and esthetic imagery of man, when he seeks to deal with process as though it means universal progress.

Wright thinks that some sort of teleology is unavoidable for an effective belief in evolutionism. It need not be the kind which supposes that all events minister to human happiness. Evolutionism is teleological by the fact that it views all events as constituting a complete and intelligible order, operating under a few original and unchanging laws. "Teleology does not consist entirely of speculations having happy *dénouements*, save that the perfection or the end to which the progress tends is a happiness to the intellect that contemplates it in its evolution and beauty of orderliness." [25] Wright is no more antagonistic than Kant or Mill toward such teleology, as long as it openly acknowledges itself to be built upon moral faith rather than scientific knowledge of nature. But whereas Spencer would like to limit the play of hopeful imagination to his preference for the evolutionary part of the evolution-dissolution cycle, Wright extends the mythic factor to the very heart of the evolutionary law as a synthetic principle in philosophy.

(4) Underlying Wright's entire polemic is his aim of keeping modern science and philosophy distinct. In criticizing Spencer, he does not detract either from Darwin's own scientific work or from the need for philosophical inquiries. Yet he does stand for what he variously calls the *neutrality* of scientific method or the nihilism of

[24] *The Philosophical Writings*, p. 21.
[25] *Loc. cit.*

modern science.[26] By these expressions he means that modern science is primarily a methodological discipline and that from its procedures and findings no consequences can be drawn for cosmology, metaphysics, ethics, and religion. Issues which belong properly in these fields cannot be given a definitive solution by appeal to biological evolution or any other scientific theory, no matter how far it is generalized.

As a scientific concept, evolution must be restricted to biology and some physiological aspects of psychology, along with the social growth of language and law. The claim for universal explanatory significance of evolutionism is not continuous with or supported by the biological position. The latter is too intimately bound up with the concrete data, problems, and hypothetical procedures of biology to permit its controlled transformation into a first principle of philosophy. And similarly, the leading concepts in physics are too closely specified by the mathematical formulas, predictive statements, and experimental situations in that area to furnish a deductive basis from which a philosophical law of evolution might be derived. This is the sense in which scientific thinking must preserve its neutrality in the face of all efforts to use its results for the resolution of philosophical issues. And if the philosopher derives the courage of his convictions only from invoking a scientific sanction for them, then Wright is ready to admit that science turns a nihilistic face toward such a project.

Owing to his grasp on the pluralism of scientific methods and the contextual meaning of scientific concepts, Wright remained skeptical

[26] C. Wright, *Philosophical Discussions* (New York: Holt, 1878), p. 403; R. B. Perry, *The Thought and Character of William James* (2 vols., Boston: Little, Brown, 1935), I, 524–28, and II, 718–21. Perry gives an interchange between Wright and William James on the former's nihilism of scientific method. Here as everywhere in treating of American philosophy since 1860, we have to return to the documents provided by Perry on James and the men surrounding him. Perry devotes a chapter (I, 474–93) to James's criticism of Spencer's "tea-table elysium" and "orgy of ambiguity," as well as James's position that the evolutionary origin of man is acceptable as long as it allows for the mind's originality and freedom.

toward the attempt of evolutionism to use biological theories as premises for metaphysical and moral inquiry. He granted the legitimacy
of questions about God, duty, and a final end, but rejected the plan
of answering them agnostically or otherwise through a philosophical
generalization of scientific evidences and concepts. On this resolute
neutrality of modern science, he appealed to Francis Bacon and might
have added the testimony of Cardinal Newman. The last essay from
his pen was a critique of "German Darwinism" or the attempt of
Haeckel and others to metaphysicize the theories of evolutionary
biology in favor of doctrinaire materialism and monism. In treating
the scientific construct or realized abstraction "*as if* it had a meaning
independently of the things which ought to determine the true limits
and precision of its meaning," such philosophical exploiters of evolution really build their systems upon the fallacy of misplaced con-
creteness (to use Whitehead's phrase) rather than upon the facts
and theories of biology.[27]

Wright is at his best when on the offensive against evolutionism
rather than when engaged in constructive philosophical work. In
philosophy, he accepts the consequences of strict phenomenalism
concerning speculative issues and prefers to reformulate philosophical
problems in terms of practical reason and moral belief. It is here
that Peirce's handling of the evolutionary theme becomes significant,
since he does attempt to draw some speculative philosophical significance from evolution without relaxing the stringency of scientific
method. He cannot avoid a clash with Wright over this issue, since
he proposes a philosophical treatment of evolution that will accord
with the scientific method and yet avoid Spencer's loose-jointed use
of force and differentiation.

As an opening wedge, Peirce suggests that there are two ways of
taking the neutrality of science. The closed sense preferred by
Wright is that the methods and concepts of science can in principle
have no consequences bearing upon the nature of things. But this is
a definitional closure of inquiry. It is not imposed from within by
scientific method itself but is stipulated for it from without by ac-

[27] C. Wright, *Philosophical Discussions*, p. 400.

ceptance of phenomenalism. The latter is a philosophical position and should not be allowed to dictate the basic scope of scientific inquiry. Wright is properly concerned to preserve the freedom of research, but this can be done satisfactorily by the methodic refusal to settle inquiry by appeal to authority. The phenomenalist postulate is either an instance of interference by authority or else is an otiose view with which scientific intelligence can readily dispense. Inquiry can reflectively discover its own method and limits, without accepting interference from the prejudgment of phenomenalism or any other extrinsic authority.

Thus Peirce recommends a second or open meaning for the neutrality of science: It must conduct its inquiry without any interference from other sources and without any advance stipulation about the ways of being and the limits of knowing. Whether or not we can use the method and findings of science to obtain some knowledge of general structures and laws in nature must be left for the actual outcome of the effort to determine. Peirce holds that we can develop some metaphysical implications through the pragmaticist analysis of scientific procedures. And evolution is one of the cardinal points of departure for such an exploratory work.

Peirce often refers to the great upheaval in scientific thinking caused by Darwin.[28] This new influence is not only a cultural fact but also has a revolutionary philosophical significance. Darwin's ideas cannot be accommodated within the conventional British framework of empiricism and mechanistic determinism. The weakness of Spencer and other previous evolutionary philosophers lies precisely in failing to recognize that Darwin has brought about a major shift in our view of nature. Peirce pinpoints the precise locations where the

---

[28] *Values in a Universe of Chance: Selected Writings of Charles S. Peirce* (1839–1914), edited by P. P. Wiener (Stanford: Stanford University Press, 1958), pp. 148–49 (against Spencer), 263, 268. Wiener's selection of materials is excellent for studying Peirce's views on scientific method and evolutionary philosophy, and will be referred to hereafter as *Values*. Most of the sources can also be found in vols. 1, 5, 6, and 7 of *Collected Papers of Charles Sanders Peirce*, edited by C. Hartshorne, P. Weiss, and A. Burks (8 vols., Cambridge, Mass.: Harvard University Press, 1931–58). A close analysis is given in the chapter on Peirce in Wiener, *Evolution and the Founders of Pragmatism*, pp. 70–96.

evolutionary perspective calls for a radical criticism of the pre-Darwinian outlook in philosophy. As far as classical empiricism is concerned, evolution represents a challenge to its nominalism and its epistemological individualism. As for a mechanist philosophy, its determinism and reductive tendency must give way before the fresh insights of evolutionary thought.

In attacking the nominalist character of British empiricism, Peirce is sufficiently confident to state his case in the form of a dilemma that one must be either a nominalistic individualist or an evolutionist.[29] For if there is any summary statement of the evolutionary conception, it is that our universe is witnessing a growth in generality or the formed regularity of structures and functions. Genetic explanation is based upon factors of comparison and continuity among individuals in an organic group, showing that there is a real, effective foundation in natural things for general laws and relations. The evolutionary mode of inquiry is also incompatible with the epistemological bias of empiricism toward the isolated individual perceiver. On the contrary, evolutionary studies concentrate upon the individual-in-context, upon the organism already really related to its existent, active environment and the rest of the species, and not merely to its private impressions. Many classical puzzles of the empiricist theory of knowledge are bound to become artificial and irrelevant in a world which recognizes the reality of general laws and the open presence of mind to a real order of natural beings.

Even before the era of relativity theory and quantum mechanics, Peirce was using evolutionary considerations to criticize the deterministic basis of strict mechanism.[30] Together with Wright, he pointed out the significant use of the statistical notion of scientific law in Maxwell's theory of gases, in population and historical studies, and in Darwin's biological work. Evolutionary research was facilitated by taking a new view of laws of nature as being capable of formula-

---

[29] *Values*, pp. 299–300; cf. 81–84. Hume is outmoded by evolutionary thought, since his standpoint in the isolated perceiver cannot explain either the evolving patterns in nature or the social development of science itself. Whitehead would accept Peirce's criticism of Hume.

[30] *Ibid.*, pp. 94–95, 174–78, 247.

tion in terms of probability statements. Taken along with Darwin's stress on chance variation, this method indicated how thorough had to be the revision of the total determinism of events as pictured in the mechanist philosophies based on classical physics. Peirce maintained that scientific laws are regular, but with limits set on the exactness and universality of what they can predict. We have to recognize the presence of real contingency and the chance factor in natural process, as well as in our scientific means of explanation. Ours is a universe having the mixed condition of *law-along-with-chance* rather than a pure state of complete determinism or utter chaos. A philosophy which formulates evolutionary laws without respecting these limitations is engaged in the hopeless task of pouring new wine into bottles that are already cracked open and discarded in biology.

The reductive tendency of philosophical mechanism is also brought under fire by Peirce. Once we become thoroughly imbued with the genetic approach of evolutionary thought, we also become dissatisfied with the attempt to reduce all events to the uniformity of nature and to treat uniformity as an ultimate, inexplicable fact. The subjective counterpart of this reductionism is Hume's appeal to custom and the laws of association as ultimate and unanalyzable principles in the mental order. From an evolutionist standpoint, we may reasonably expect that the uniform aspects in nature also have a history, that they too have a genesis. The uniformity of nature is not an ultimate fact but an achievement which is still in process of being brought about.

If we take a fresh look at the world, instead of floating along on the tide of conventional mechanism, we are impressed that "everywhere the main fact is growth and increasing complexity." [31] The variety and diversity and constant growth of kinds of things reveal the presence of spontaneity at the heart of nature, as Darwin himself had suggested in his law of constant divergence of species. There is objective chance in the sense of variescence or the collective tendency to variableness. Peirce has his own doctrine of tychism or recogni-

[31] *Ibid.*, p. 174; cf. pp. 217, 429.

tion of the inexpugnable chance factor in the universe, but he also warns against forgetting the inductive basis for the affirmation of chance and thus paying superstitious homage to it. Used in a critical way, however, the stress on spontaneity and chance as real ingredients in things helps us to see the developmental character of natural laws or the evolutionary tendency toward stable patterns of activity. Far from being a brute, unanalyzable postulate, the uniformity of nature is genetically intelligible as the drift toward law, the tendency of the universe to increase the habit of regular and generalized modes of action.

After using evolutionary ideas to undermine nominalism, empiricism, and mechanism, Peirce then employs them in constructing his own cosmogony and metaphysics. His evolutionary explanation

would suppose that in the beginning—infinitely remote—there was a chaos of unpersonalized feeling, which being without connection or regularity would properly be without existence. This feeling, sporting here and there in pure arbitrariness, would have started the germ of a generalizing tendency. Its other sportings would be evanescent, but this would have a growing virtue. Thus, the tendency to habit would be started; and from this with the other principles of evolution all the regularities of the universe would be evolved.[32]

This account is offered as a probable hypothesis requiring future verification, not as a demonstrative proof. One of Peirce's critics, Arthur O. Lovejoy, has objected that we never could verify the initial condition of pure spontaneity without introducing determinations into it, and that there would be no reasonable ground for expecting an initial condition of promiscuous diversity ever to develop a tendency to depart from purely random variations. But Peirce suggests that his evidence is not to be sought by dreaming oneself back to an evolutionary start but rather by analyzing the presently experienced variety, random tendency, and uniformity. And he describes the

[32] Values, pp. 158–59. A. O. Lovejoy's criticism is found as Appendix E, in Wiener's Evolution and the Founders of Pragmatism, pp. 227–30. Peirce had already replied to Paul Carus' similar objection by noting that the initial condition is "an indefinite specifiability, which is nothing but a tendency to the diversification of the nothing."—Peirce, Collected Papers, 6.612.

original indeterminate state not as a homogeneity but as a heterogeneity of indefinite specifiability, virtually involving in its dynamism
two tendencies which we can actually see in our world: that toward
novelty and that toward continuous formation of laws. The latter is
a growing tendency, however, so that the laws and regularity now
prevailing are themselves an evolutionary achievement.

Peirce is now prepared to give a thoroughly evolutionary definition of what the scientist calls a law of nature:

> So, then, I do not think a better definition of a *law of nature* can be
> given than this: it is a foreknowing generalization of observations. This
> said, the question is instantly started, How can the reason of a man
> attain such foreknowledge? How shall we answer? Must we not say that
> the fact that he can so attain proves that there is an energizing reason-
> ableness that shapes phenomena in some sense, and that this same work-
> ing reasonableness has molded the reason of man into something like its
> own image? [33]

This is a pregnant text for understanding the mind of Peirce and
measuring the depth of his evolutionary way of thinking. He begins
with a fact of scientific description: We do possess some knowledge
that is inductive or observationally based, that involves a predictive
factor, and that is held in a generalized form. In asking about the
basis rendering this fact possible, he does not appeal to some permanent Kantian forms of the consciousness in general but rather to an
evolutionary process of energizing and molding. Moreover, it is a
growth in reasonableness, in so far as our world shows an increasing
tendency to take on the characters of generality, continuity, and feasible form. They are the objective marks of law as a reasonableness
energizing in the world, even though it is working under the limiting
conditions of chance and contingency.

This growth of reasonableness is transpiring not only in the world
but also in the human mind, to the extent that scientific inquiry is
bringing it gradually more into responsive conformity with the living

[33] *Values*, p. 291; cf. 300, 316. The context for this definition is an essay
on "The Laws of Nature and Hume's Argument against Miracles," which, as
the accompanying correspondence reveals, was composed under frustrating intellectual and financial conditions for S. P. Langley of the Smithsonian Institution.

and developing pattern of generality in nature. Thus the evolution of law is a complex process occurring both in natural events and structures and in the scientifically progressing mind of man. The natural universe is just as thoroughly temporal and historical as is the human world. Far from regarding his theory of the evolutionary beginning and the genesis of law in nature as a hindrance to theism, Peirce employs the harmony devolping between the reasonableness of things and that of human inquiry as evidence of God's effective and providential presence in the universe.

All of the main doctrines in Peirce's philosophy have an evolutionary significance. It permeates his theory of method, doctrine of the categories, cosmology, scientific ethics, and even his account of the history of science. The common evolutionary ambience for all the parts of his philosophy can be indicated even in a brief description.

Thus in his theory of scientific method, Peirce stresses the role of hypothesis-forming or abduction. It has a spontaneous aspect corresponding to the spontaneity in developing nature. Yet responsible hypothesizing is never arbitrary but seeks to bear in a relevant way upon the data and problems at hand, as well as to submit itself to a continuing public verification by the scientific community. This abductive search after increasingly relevant and verified hypotheses is an instance of the growth of reasonableness on the part of the human inquirer, more specifically on the part of the scientific community as a whole. There is a growth of law as a firm and continuous pattern both in natural events and in scientific research, although contingency and revisibility remain in force in both areas. The reason why Peirce thinks that his remarks on the habit-taking tendency in nature do not constitute a mere extrapolation of psychology is that he finds a common evolutionary structure governing the logic of abduction and the course of natural events.

His theory of the three basic categories remains obscure unless there is some reference to its evolutionary import. It takes a triadic form, not because of the influence of Hegel but because of the predominance of the evolutionary model taken from biology and the analysis of scientific method. Every situation can be analyzed into its genetic source, its finalizing aim, and its continuous approach toward that end. This provides Peirce with his primary categories of an indeterminate possibility or undifferentiated feeling, a generality of final structure, and a mediating process of habit-taking which generates the directional movement from source toward a generalized goal.

The basic categorial scheme can then be used interpretatively in cosmology and ethics. Since Peirce defines the real in terms of the trend toward increased regularity and embodied or steadied generality, he regards the evolutionary flow quite literally as a continuous realizing of the natural world. This realization process can be given a categorial analysis. For the becoming of things must involve three cosmic traits: chance, the love and pursuit of generality, and the continuity of process between them.

Tychism or the doctrine on chance is an affirmation of the factor of spontaneity and contingency in all natural happening. Agapism or the doctrine on the love and pursuit of general structures defends the antinominalistic thesis that general factors are really present in nature and are constantly in course of being further actualized. And synechism or the doctrine on continuity seeks to explain the oriented character of the real as movement from the indeterminate to structured determinateness, from private feeling to publicly verified and commonly held knowledge. Peirce attaches these somewhat outlandish Greek names to his cosmological principles in order to signify a unique evolutionary standpoint which is reducible neither to the Hegelian dialectical triad nor to biological evolution apart from rigorous logical analysis of method.

He adds that agapism has a moral as well as a cosmic meaning, for it helps to define the purpose of human efforts. The pragmaticist or scientific philosopher must seek to embody generality or the network of regular and continuous patterns in his thought and action, corresponding to a similar tendency in nature. This is nothing less than saying that the well-disciplined mind finds its moral enthusiasm and direction in promoting evolution in the properly human sphere of mind, cultural response, and methodic control.

Accordingly, the pragmaticist does not make the *summum bonum* to consist in action, but makes it to consist in that process of evolution whereby the existent comes more and more to embody those generals which were just now said to be *destined*, which is what we strive to express in calling them *reasonable*. In its higher stages, evolution takes place more and more largely through self-control, and this gives the pragmaticist a sort of justification for making the rational purport to be general.[34]

This text contains a correction of the pragmatism of James precisely by interpreting the aim of evolution in function of increasing generality rather than action. By anticipation, it also criticizes that sort of existentialist stress which would divorce the existent from the reasonable and the general. As Peirce views the problem, to make such a divorce would be nothing less than to unmake the real and to reduce the existent to the purely possible, in a word, to strip man and the universe of their proper evolutionary tendency.

At the semicentennial celebration of Darwin's work held at Columbia University, John Dewey spoke on his influence upon philosophy. This is one of Dewey's most personally intended papers, since he himself was born in 1859 and made the pilgrimage from idealism to instrumental naturalism under the growing pressure of Darwinian thought. Especially the suggestions of Darwin and Wallace concerning human emotional and intellectual development sapped his confidence in the doctrine of an immanent absolute spirit as the source and standard of human life. Dewey's initial idealism was unsettled also by the juxtaposition of "origin" and "species" in the very title of Darwin's masterwork. This meant that the essential and the fixed were giving way to the temporal and the fluid in the biological and

[34] *Values*, p. 199. Peirce retained several theories of evolution in order to account for the several ways in which science advances: by chance discovery (Darwin), by persistent habitual effort (Lamarck), and by the violent influx of new evidence upsetting the old habits of thought (Clarence King, the American geologist). Thus he gave a plurimodal evolutionary explanation of the history of science itself (*Ibid.*, pp. 149–50, 257–60).

human worlds, as well as in that of physics. For Dewey, the chief significance of Darwin was to justify a universal extension of the genetic viewpoint and thus to banish everywhere in nature the notion of a fixed ladder of being or hierarchy of forms.

But Dewey himself went on from the continuity and genetic descent of species established by evolutionary biology to urge that the process constitutes a self-sufficient whole of nature and excludes as meaningless the problem of the being and providential care of a God distinct from evolutionary nature. "Once admit that the sole verifiable or fruitful object of knowledge is the particular set of changes that generate the object of study together with the consequences that then flow from it, and no intelligible question can be asked about what, by assumption, lies outside." [35] This methodological restriction of meaningful issues to events in change was a philosophical addition made on Dewey's own responsibility to clear the way for his naturalistic theory of man and experience. This is clear from the weight he imparted to the operative phrase "the sole verifiable or fruitful object of knowledge." From Darwin's cautious agnosticism, he could not gather any such general and restrictive pronouncement about the object of knowledge, but only a description of what constitutes the business of the biologist.

Both Peirce and Dewey engage in methodological and metaphysical generalization on the theme of evolution. But in the former case, it is clearer that a distinctive philosophical analysis is being made and a new hypothesis being proposed for common testing. Dewey tends to consolidate his naturalistic interpretation with the biological meaning for evolution and evolutionary research, as though naturalism in philosophy is only a further chapter in the same line as the biological findings. Hence his account of Darwin's significance is more instructive as the story of how a new attitude in philosophy is born in a

[35] J. Dewey, *The Influence of Darwin on Philosophy and Other Essays in Contemporary Thought* (reprint ed., New York: Peter Smith, 1951), p. 14. See M. G. White, *The Origin of Dewey's Instrumentalism* (New York: Columbia University Press, 1943), pp. 109–25, on his early struggle with evolution. Its bearing on his naturalism is traced by J. Collins, "The Genesis of Dewey's Naturalism," in *John Dewey: His Thought and Influence*, edited by John Blewett, S.J. (New York: Fordham University Press, 1960), pp. 1–32.

Darwinian atmosphere than as the strict justification of how this philosophy comes to close off an entire area of inquiry as being without meaning.

4. BERGSON AND THE METHODOLOGY OF EVOLUTIONISM

Among the more prominent twentieth-century thinkers who can be regarded as philosophers of evolution are Samuel Alexander, Alfred North Whitehead, and Henri Bergson. The theme emerges with purity and dominance in the mind of Bergson, but in the other men it is blended with many other considerations, especially those arising from relativity theory and the search for a world of values. Here, we can confine ourselves to a brief examination of some aspects in Bergson's philosophical position. It remains closer to the biologist's approach to nature and to the actual shifts in evolutionary theories, without surrendering the human significance of the genesis of life.

We have already mentioned Bergson's criticism of the concept of force in Spencer's system. As a beginner in philosophy (the Bergson centenary was also in 1959), he thought that Spencer was basically sound and needed only to be provided with a more rigorous mathematico-mechanical notion of force. But to his surprise, Bergson soon found [36] that even this addition was insufficient to close the gap between the Spencerian formula for change and change as we experience it in its temporal reality. And since time is of the essence for every evolutionary theory, Bergson had to look for another way of bringing a philosophy of evolution into conformity with our temporal experi-

[36] H. Bergson, *The Creative Mind* (New York: Philosophical Library, 1946), pp. 10–13; H. Bergson, *Creative Evolution* (New York: Modern Library, 1944), pp. 395–402. The latter work concludes with a criticism of Spencer's mechanist or extrinsic method and an affirmation of Bergson's own internal method. "It is within the evolutionary movement that we place ourselves, in order to follow it to its present results, instead of recomposing these results artificially with fragments of themselves. . . . It is the study of becoming in general, it is true evolutionism and consequently the true continuation of science" in the Bergsonian philosophy of duration.—*Creative Evolution*, p. 402. On the grounds for reading Darwin teleologically with Bergson rather than mechanistically with Dewey, see G. Himmelfarb, *Darwin and the Darwinian Revolution* (New York: Doubleday, 1959), 325–30. But Himmelfarb does not distinguish clearly enough between Darwin's own outlook and limitations and those of his later interpreters.

ence. His original contributions in philosophy arose from this need to provide a more adequate generalized theory of evolution than any which was based on the notion of time in classical mechanics. In his sensitivity toward the limitations of the Newtonian outlook not so much on physical grounds as on those of human experience, he resembled Peirce.

What is inadequate about the ordinary notion of time which is found in most of the uncritical conceptions of evolution? The fact that it is modeled after the concept of space, that it is only an echo of spatial conditions. We tend to conceive of time as a series of point-instants which stretch out homogeneously in a line, one discrete instant succeeding the other in a set groove, like raindrops rolling down a gutter. Bergson does not maintain that this spatializing of time is false or useless: it does serve the practical purpose of scientific prediction and control. His criticism is directed against erecting this practical purpose into the sole norm for our thinking about time. If we do so, we fail to respect the biologist's report on the inner spontaneity, continuity of action, and speciating divergence of temporal organisms. Above all, we fail to do justice to our own experience of temporal duration which refuses to conform with the spatial pattern of points on a pre-existent and fully determined linear course. Any notion of time which is in discrepancy with these approaches to temporal duration cannot be used in a reliable philosophy of evolution. The negative conclusion is that we will have to refrain from using the physicalized view of time in our description of evolutionary process.

Bergson thus involves himself in the recurrent problem of how to make a warranted generalization of evolutionary traits set forth in biological research. His answer is given in the methodological resolve to deal with evolution as far as possible within a humanly experienceable context and to resist explaining away the data of that experience in terms of anything else. The biological findings of Darwin and his successors do not arrange themselves automatically into a philosophical doctrine on the evolutionary nature of life. The only route for attaining a cosmic meaning of evolution is by close study of our human experience of duration, not because we fear dehumanization but because we can perhaps find the general nature of the evolutionary process as it is brought to conscious awareness in man.[37] For Bergson, it is not a question of anthropomorphizing evolution but rather of seizing it as an ongoing process in the region where it is most accessible to us: in our experience of the self as a spontaneous durational act. The details of Bergson's account, in *Creative Evolution*, of the branchings of the various evolutionary lines are ultimately not as important as his presentation of the *methodological* problem. Some of the more recent philosophical treatments of evolution seem to be more placidly inevitable than his, but this is often due to their way of gliding over the crucial point of how to develop the concepts of biological evolution into a reliable and illuminating philosophy of evolution.

Unlike most proponents of evolutionism, Bergson is uneasy about the procedure of interpreting the evolutionary process in terms of either classical or relativity physics.[38] He is unable to make the kind of synthesis which Alexander and Whitehead regard as inevitable between the evolutionary and the physical standpoints of our age. His difficulty stems not only from the problem of physicalized time but also from the nature of human experience stipulated within the physical system. In Newtonian physics there is an absolute system of reference, and once the privileged observer is installed therein, it is indifferent to him whether other real observers exist and whether his own experience contains anything beyond the data relevant for the system itself. In relativity theory, the given real observer supposes that other systems of reference are occupied by other observers, but

[37] Scholastic critics were sometimes arguing at cross purposes with Bergson, since his doctrine on intuition and more fluid concepts was not inspired primarily by anti-intellectualism in the broad meaning of intelligence but by a positive effort to reach the heart of evolutionary reality through an attention to life in its temporal course. "The movement will not be grasped from without and, as it were, from where I am, but from within, inside it, in what it is in itself."— *The Creative Mind*, p. 188.

[38] Bergson has been criticized for his remarks on relativity theory, but sometimes without seeing that his main purpose was to show that present physical theory neither supports nor attacks his philosophy of evolutionary duration. Cf. *ibid.*, pp. 301–03, n. 5.

he does not have assurance of their actuality and his own interest does not extend beyond the requirements for space-time predictions.

But Bergson requires of the inductive basis for an evolutionary philosophy that it consist of the self-experience of several actual individuals, that it faithfully report these individuals' durational reality in its own being and not simply as a function of the space-time system, and that it seize upon the direction of life. Such conditions cannot be met by the abstraction called the physical observer but only by the concrete man in his reflective durational experience. Thus the Bergsonian intuition of duration is not intended as a flight from intelligence or from ordinary experience; it is the methodologically unavoidable instrument for gaining the sort of inductive data which can be generalized into an evolutionary philosophy.

What Bergson encounters in his interior exploration of lived duration is the vital impetus or the struggle of freedom moving in a spiritual direction toward God and against the eddies and obstacles of matter. This result has never appeared very convincing to biologists. In his Eddington Memorial Lecture, the pioneer geneticist R. A. Fisher rejects Bergson's vital impetus as a piece of mythological dualism which explains none of the particular evolutionary phenomena.[39] Bergson would have to admit that we cannot derive any statistical laws of gene mutation from his position and that it does not provide guidance in setting up a biological experiment. However, he would probably add that its purpose is not to render the biologist's initiative superfluous but to state some general and yet concrete meaning for the life process.

His plane of approach can be appreciated by considering the two-fold sense in which Fisher himself admits a valid meaning for "creative evolution." It signifies effective causation, along with the achieving of new and important results through the activities of liv-

[39] R. A. Fisher, *Creative Aspects of Natural Law* (Cambridge: Cambridge University Press, 1950), pp. 4–6 (his meaning for creative evolution), 6–11, 14–15 (on Bergson). Fisher is more sympathetic toward the holistic doctrine propounded by J. C. Smuts, *Holism and Evolution* (London: Macmillan, 1926). Smuts deliberately left the philosophical elaboration of his position to others, however, and hence did not face the full brunt of the evolutionary problem at the level of methodology.

ing beings. The philosophical problems concern both the nature of the causation common to all living things and the meaning to be assigned to the judgment that a certain achievement is important. Bergson's suggestion is that our durational activity conveys a common meaning for evolutionary causation which is not reducible to statistical statement and spatial imagery. Furthermore, a philosophical signification for what is important in evolutionary activity can be obtained by including a reference to our own maximal becoming in the direction of freedom and spiritual self-possession. This result is meager enough, but Bergson will insist that anyone who is searching for the philosophical meaning of evolution must at least proceed in this way for his answer.

Bergson was engaged neither in deducing the genetic theory of life nor in answering the questions of classical metaphysics. His chief concern was to determine how we can establish the wider implications of evolution. His approach through our experience of duration was inevitably psychological, so that he came to regard matter as sluggish imagery and to defend evolutionary progress by appeal to memory as a prolonging into the vital present. Within his own context, there are two further methodological questions which have to be formulated more clearly than he saw fit to do. Does biological evolution in fact contain any quite general metaphysical implications about the whole cosmic process and the full sweep of the nature of life? And if so, does our human experience of temporal duration and freedom lead to the core of the vital process or only to a special case, which is too narrow for such generalization? Philosophers of evolution answer the first question in the affirmative, but the sense is that here is a program to be tried out so that we can eventually test it by the results of particular efforts to reach the general meaning of evolution. This leads at once to the problem of method, and on this score Bergson presses hard for our taking reasonable advantage of our own reflective presence in the evolutionary field. Even after this is faithfully done, however, the difficulty remains of correlating the distinctively human meaning for vital operations with those which the biologists and other workers gather through their own methods.

5. THREE IDEALISTIC APPRAISALS OF EVOLUTION

Not all the young idealists followed Dewey supinely into disillusionment with their metaphysical position and eventual repudiation of the main tenets of idealism. There were at least three types of idealistic response which involved no capitulation to naturalism but rather a vigorous effort to welcome Darwinism within the mansions of idealism. Royce's method was to engulf the whole evolutionary doctrine within the capacious arms of the absolute self. On behalf of a more personal idealism, Howison stressed the limits of evolutionary explanation in respect to the human self. And more recently, Harris has used the resources of the logic of science to reinstate an idealistic basis for the evolutionary view of things.

Josiah Royce testifies to the powerful challenge of evolution by devoting the entire second half of *The Spirit of Modern Philosophy* to this question. His first aim is to explain historically the eager acceptance and rapid application of Darwin's ideas. They could not have been so readily assimilated in the earlier periods of the rationalist static dualism of mind and body or the equally static skepticism of the empiricist mind, but only in the idealistic phase of modern philosophy. Schelling and Hegel have accustomed us to think of the spiritual absolute as being in constant development, to view nature as alive with this divine presence and process, and to approach all special problems in terms of the history of the subject in question. Thus idealism has tilled the soil for the enthusiastic welcome given to evolutionary views.

Royce is not blind to the defects in the view of nature found among the German idealists. No naturalistic critic speaks more bitingly than he about the grotesqueries of the Romantic and Hegelian philosophies of nature. But he locates their failure not in their metaphysical principles but in their inability to adhere rigorously by these principles in treating of empirical events. Granted that the source and subject of the orderly course of phenomenal objects is the infinite self or absolute spirit, it does not follow that our ideas under the conditions of human limitation are perfect enough to provide an *a priori* deductive basis for the study of nature. The mind of the idealistic philosopher is itself in process of growth: it requires a temporal process to discover the manifestations of the absolute self. Hence the well-disciplined idealist must accept the phenomena of nature as they come, forswearing any impatient schemes of anticipating their meaning by the manipulation of a symbolism or a dialectic.

Yet the idealist also possesses another perspective on nature, based on his confidence that

the Self is as truly present in evolution as he is in sin and ignorance. These are the World-Spirit's garments that we see him by . . . [but] only after a patient scientific scrutiny has revealed, as is the case with the doctrine of evolution, a vast unity in a long series of phenomena. . . . I rather delight in this craft whereby the Self thus hides its true nature in energetic nebulous masses and in flying meteors, pretends to be absent from the inorganic world, pretends to have descended from relatives of the anthropoid apes, pretends, in short, to be bounded in all sorts of nutshells.[40]

The very thoroughness and comprehensiveness of scientific evolutionary research raise the further question of the principle of unity for the whole series of living things. The Roycean reply is that all vital phenomena are the garments or manifestations of the one absolute self, which synthesizes them into a meaningful pattern for our investigation. There is even a certain playfulness or pretense in nature, in so far as the empirical forms do not immediately reveal the presence of the infinite self but seem to hide it. This provides a challenge not only for the scientist, who must find some proximate

[40] *The Spirit of Modern Philosophy*, pp. 306, 307. The repetition of the word "pretends" is reminiscent of Hegel on the cunning of reason, as is the reference to sin and ignorance. For an adjustment of Hegel's theory of the contingent and irrational factors in nature with Darwin on the variability in natural selection, read D. G. Ritchie, *Darwin and Hegel* (New York: Macmillan, 1893), pp. 56–58.

pattern of rationality, but also for the philosopher in his quest for a general interpretation of the life process.

Royce takes a clue from Peirce on how to use some scientific notions as aids toward reaching a satisfactory philosophical account of evolution.[41] There is a describable common tendency in nature and human affairs to form aggregates or statistically definable groups, to exert some natural selection at the group level, and to form habits which strengthen some older aggregates and engender some new ones. Behind the biological theory of evolution lies the logic of *aggregates*. The evolutionary law is that there is fecundity in whatever unites for orderly cooperation. Persons and bodies share in the evolutionary trend in so far as they join in promoting the welfare of a community, whether it be a spiritual or a physical one. The reason for the prevailing pattern of the logic of aggregates is that it is the common way in which the absolute spirit expresses itself in nature and man.

To clinch the idealistic interpretation of evolution, Royce adds that all aggregates are serial order-systems, which are types of cosmic selves. Their internal principle of unity is the effective presence of some ideal which the individual members in the group or serial system are striving to realize. A self is simply a well-ordered series whose components are endeavoring to achieve a condition of activity and control through a continuum of evolutionary forms. Thus mountain ranges and biological species are cosmic selves having a different time span from each other and from the human individual self. Evolution is the pattern of interconnection and communication between these social order-systems, all of which are types of conscious processes of self-expression. Evolutionary law unifies all the aggregates on both a cosmic and an individual basis, thus enabling the absolute self to bring about the great community of material and spiritual agencies. The evolutionary law of self-representing aggregates is the

[41] Royce develops these views in *The World and the Individual* (2 vols., New York: Macmillan, 1900–01), I, 501 ff., and II, 209–33, 315–23; "The Mechanical, the Historical and the Statistical," *Science*, N. S., XXXIX (1914), 551–66. He wants to demonstrate the idealistic hypothesis that evolutionary laws of irreversible processes "*are in their most general type, common to Matter and to Mind, to the physical and to the moral world.*"—*The World and the Individual*, II, 218.

means employed by the absolute to achieve continuity, similarity, and ultimately cooperative activity throughout natural and human history. Royce attaches to this interpretation of evolution the warning that it cannot be used deductively to establish or test the empirical theories in biology but only to give them a context of meaning and unity with the laws discovered for other order-systems in our universe.

While Royce was lecturing to his Boston and Cambridge audiences on how to incorporate evolution within the doctrine of the absolute, George Howison was building a case at the University of California for personal idealism against both evolutionary pragmatism and absolute idealism. He criticized the former position for its psychological use of evolution and its analysis of continuity in the universe. Instead of following Royce's absolutism of the infinite self, he found a basis in Kant and the inviolable human person from which to establish some limits for evolutionary thought.

Dewey had assumed that the *a priori* factor in knowledge is easily discredited by showing that our ideas and mental forms are the outcome of evolutionary process. Howison did not deny the legitimacy of a genetic description of thought, but he stressed the distinction between the psychological growth of a conception and its meaning and validity. The two latter questions are not settled simply by recounting the genesis of our thought. The evolutionary psychologizing of the forms of thought tends to confuse the feeling of being necessitated in our acts of mind with the perception of a necessary connection of meaning in the objects of thought.[42] One must also inquire about the general principles of thought which make it possible for us to have the associative bonds upon which a genetic psychology relies. Although he was lacking in the systematic range and penetration of Husserl, Howison took a similar stand against any attempt to convert an evolutionary description of the development of our thinking into a standard for judging its validity.

Another problem which he illuminates is the shift of meaning

[42] *George Holmes Howison, Philosopher and Teacher: A Selection from His Writings with a Biographical Sketch,* by J. W. Buckham and G. M. Stratton (Berkeley: University of California Press, 1934), pp. 163–64, 184.

when we pass from the biological to the philosophical meaning of evolution. Biological evolution "means not only *logical* community, or resemblance for observation and thought, but also likeness due to descent and birth; due to a *physiological* community, through the process of reproduction." [43] But when we start speaking about evolution as a cosmic process, we have to weaken or eliminate the note of physiological community, in any definite biological and causal sense, and content ourselves with the thread of logical community. Howison grants that this is a perfectly legitimate act of the mind, but it has some consequences which pragmatic naturalism does not see. The generalized method of genetic and comparative research can be applied in all fields, but the success of its application does not warrant the inference that therefore all things are related solely by the immanent continuity and causal descent required for the naturalistic self-sufficient whole of being. The logical meaning for continuity of analysis cannot be made the premise for drawing a metaphysical conclusion about the real being and relatedness of the objects of analysis. The only way to do this is to coalesce the physiological and logical meanings for community, and such a coalescence empties out the biological theory from which we make our start.

The only thread of continuity between the different meanings for community and genetic descent is a logical one, a unity of congruous interpretative conceptions and not a naturalistic monism of real process. To attain a generalized evolutionism, we must not only make an extrapolation from paleontology and biology but also perform this act with the distinctive resources of the human mind. The life of the investigating human mind is one irreducible source for philosophical evolutionism. And against Royce, Howison defends the irreducibility of the individual intelligence of men to modes of an absolute self. Human minds do join cooperatively in the community of scientific research, but they remain personal centers and never become sheer manifestations of some overself. That they are not self-sufficient beings is seen from their receptivity in regard to sensation and their obligation under moral law, but this means that

[43] *Ibid.*, p. 169; cf. 177.

men stand open to the ideals and the activity of a personal God. Howison does not import evolutionary development into God, however, but confines it to the natural, nonpersonal world. Men are not related to the divine in the manner of evolutionary waves (as Samuel Alexander depicts the situation) but as finite persons to the personal, self-possessed being of God.

Howison's confining of evolution to nature as a nonpersonal realm depended in principle, however, upon the Kantian distinction between phenomena (the evolutionary events and laws in nature) and noumena (the personal, nonevolving being of man and God). Since this distinction is now widely challenged by analytic and naturalistic philosophies, more recent proponents of idealism are looking for approaches based more closely upon the logic of current science. This brings them much closer to Royce's plan of assimilating evolution to absolute idealism through a study of the implications of scientific concepts. This is the path followed by Errol Harris in his book *Nature, Mind, and Modern Science*.

A good portion of this work is devoted to showing that classical empiricism and logical positivism are dead ends which cannot establish with rigor their principle for the verifiability of meaning.[44] Hence they cannot advance any *a priori* objections against the project of an idealistic interpretation of evolution on the ground that it is a metaphysical, and hence an intrinsically meaningless, enterprise. This easy solution founders on the fact that the operations of hypothesizing, relating, and classifying which belong to any scientific work, including the biological theory of evolution, involve much more than the registration of present sense contents. The establishing of connections between hypotheses and empirical data involves too many factors to permit logical positivism to maintain its criterion of empirical meaning as a definite bar against metaphysical studies of scientific concepts.

Thus Harris wants to reopen the idealistic examination of evolution after the pause induced by the logical positivists and empiricists.

[44] E. Harris, *Nature, Mind, and Modern Science* (New York: Macmillan, 1954), pp. 328–55.

Yet he refuses to accept Driesch's entelechy, since it is too vague, extrinsic, and dualistic to explain satisfactorily the traits of the organism. Instead, he proposes that the concrete universal of Hegel can be reinterpreted as realizing itself in organic things and constituting their internal telic principle. Embryonic development is a dialectical type of process, wherein an undifferentiated potentiality is polarized with a specializing differentiation of parts, leading to a final synthesis of unity in diversity or an integrated complex whole, the organism. The only adequate philosophical analysis of the facts of integrative growth is furnished by the immanent concrete universal.

The modern scientific outlook and its evolutionary biology contain a fivefold set of implications for philosophy.[45] (1) Nature constitutes a single system in which there are no sharp breaks between matter, life, and mind. Harris remarks that, for absolute idealism, the primacy of mind is not based on a static dualism of mind and body but on the teleological principle that all roads of development lead eventually to mind as their supreme concretion. (2) Evolution is not only change but directional growth, not only efficient causation but final as well. Indeed, these types of causation tend to overlap and converge in such a way that events are adequately explained only through an evolutionary teleology. (3) We do not look for the telic completion of an evolutionary process in something isolated and apart from developing nature but precisely in the climax of all organic wholes: the minded organism. Philosophically considered, mind or the final cause is immanently present in nature from the outset and exerts a controlling influence over all stages in the evolutionary movement. Evolution is progressive in so far as the immanent concrete universal constantly tends toward its realization in mind or the plenary instance of unity amid diversity.

(4) Because all of nature has mind as its dynamic internal principle, the long-standing epistemological split between subject and object, mind and thing, is overcome. Man recognizes their ultimate identity when he experiences and reflects upon the outcome of evolution in his own mode of being, which is the natural world brought

[45] *Ibid.*, pp. 202–06, 373–74.

to conscious activity. The biologist's working conviction that the evolutionary process is intelligible and will yield definite results to research is thereby justified on the idealistic basis of the presence of mind or the rational principle in and as the forms of organic development. (5) Finally, a natural world whose evolution is a journey toward conscious mind cannot be a world deprived of value and real qualities, as the empiricist generalizers of Galilean mechanics presumed. Harris defends the actual presence of qualities and values in the evolving world as being more in harmony with the convictions of evolutionary theorists. Their appeal to survival value is not groundless, but it does require a justification and finds it in idealism. Survival value is only a preliminary way of stating that the valuable is that which promotes remotely or proximately the fuller realization of mind in nature and mind's active control over natural process.

Harris admits that these five points do not completely restore the metaphysics of absolute idealism. The implications drawn from evolutionary biology do not extend beyond the minded organism or mind in the human condition. Furthermore, the biological viewpoint does not establish the unitary convergence of all lines of evolution upon the human organism as the synthesizing telic principle of every evolutionary path. As supplementary evidence, then, Harris singles out the human mind's capacity to embrace the entire temporal flow of evolution in a reflective concept. Time's domain extends as far as bodies and animate processes, but then the temporal process gets comprehended as a whole and thus gets transcended by conscious mind. Yet our developing, fallible, finite minds do not achieve the full consciousness and perfect grasp of all phases of evolution as required by the unconditional telic actuality or concrete universal. "Consequently, the complete manifestation of the universal in a perfect mind is the inescapable presupposition of all science and all thought based upon the concept of evolution." [46] Without perhaps realizing it, therefore, the evolutionist is providing data whose ultimate significance requires acceptance of the absolute mind.

Harris adds that this is the real foundation for the ontological

[46] *Nature, Mind, and Modern Science*, p. 442.

argument, which is now continuous with a thorough analysis of evolutionary findings. Yet evolutionary thought furnishes a support for the ontological argument *to* God only when the evolutionary course is viewed idealistically as the immanent development *of* the absolute mind itself. Hence this analysis of modern biology does not lead to God in the theistic sense but rather to the developing absolute of a renovated Hegelian idealism. That is why Harris admits efficient causality only in order to fuse it completely with an immanent teleology and thus rule out any inference to a transcendent God by means of efficient cause.

Some obscurities continue to surround this renovation of dialectical absolutism. Harris does not show how the Hegelian notion of a scale of forms can be revised to mean a transformation of forms through descent or how there is any scientific warrant for maintaining a transformation from the minded organism to the absolute mind. He also leaves in the dark his crucial distinction between the temporal process of bodies and animate structures and what he calls the "timeless analytic-synthetic discursus" of self-conscious mind.[47] Temporality becomes only a preliminary manifestation of the concrete universal, whose true and abiding actuality is timeless. It is not sufficient to say that the reality of time is respected by treating timeless reflection as a terminal development. For in an absolute idealism, the timeless concrete universal is also the intimate principle and value standard which gives meaning and being to the temporal events as its own aspects or phases. We are left wondering whether temporal process can be anything more than a reflected play of graduated formal concepts, and hence whether the evolution studied by biologists is ever really dealt with in terms of the idealistic theory of an immanently developing timeless discursus.

6. Julian Huxley's Evolutionary Humanism

During the 1958–59 centenary meetings as well as during the past generation, the most energetic champion of a philosophical human-

[47] *Loc. cit.*

ism built upon Darwinism has been Sir Julian Huxley. He performed yeoman scientific service during the lean years when Darwin
himself was in eclipse and when it required considerable staying
power to defend natural selection. After the work of Fisher, Haldane,
and Muller showed that the genetic mechanism could be related to
the factors of adaptation and selection, Huxley took the lead in combining the new genetics with Darwinism to give the modified position now generally held. Huxley showed convincingly that Neo-
Darwinism provides a unifying principle for all the sub-areas in
biology and a fruitful guide for continuing research. In addition,
he contended that the evolutionary position can be expanded into a
total philosophy for understanding the universe and guiding men in
their valuational choices. Although his philosophical evolutionism
did not receive the same wide allegiance among biologists, it was
welcomed by many philosophical naturalists and humanists as scientific confirmation of their notion of self-sufficing nature and purely
immanent values for man.

Huxley distinguishes formally between evolution as a mechanism
of genetic and natural selection agencies and evolution as a process
or the ongoing result of the operation of the agencies.[48] They are
related not only descriptively but also causally: The selective-genetic
mechanism is a real efficient cause and the process or course of evolutionary change is its real effect and product. Huxley thus takes the
decisive step of treating the description of selective and adaptive situations and the mathematical analysis of gene factors as genuine

---

[48] See his essay on "The Evolutionary Process," in *Evolution as a Process*,
edited by J. Huxley, A. C. Hardy, and E. B. Ford (London: Allen and Unwin,
1954), pp. 1–13. The factual data and theories in the various sciences supporting
the Neo-Darwinian account of evolution are presented by G. G. Simpson, *The
Meaning of Evolution* (New Haven: Yale University Press, 1949); W. K. Gregory,
Evolution Emerging (2 vols., New York: Macmillan, 1951); L. C. Cuénot,
L'évolution biologique (Paris: Masson, 1951). In their concluding sections,
Simpson and Gregory take a position close to the naturalism and evolutionary
humanism of Julian Huxley, yet Gregory holds that evolutionary steps are irrevocable but not irreversible. Cuénot is even more cautious and does not
absolutize the evolutionary factors. Huxley's address on "Man and the Future of
Evolution" dominated the Chicago centennial meeting; cf. S. Tax (ed.), *Evolution after Darwin* (3 vols. Chicago: University of Chicago Press, 1960).

causal statements, and indeed as the biological expression of evolutionary process or the sole causal agency in things. He does not argue this point but simply finds it just as customary as did his grandfather, Thomas Huxley, to speak about evolutionary principles as the true causes.

His next concern is to describe the evolutionary causes as being creative, mechanical, and progressive. Each of these qualifications is given a distinctive meaning in the Huxleyan context, although he offers his philosophical analysis as though it were the common heritage of all biologists.

"Creative" has the negative sense of excluding any more ultimate causal source outside of nature and the positive sense of producing real and basic results in nature. Julian Huxley moves far beyond the minimal agnostic position of Darwin and Thomas Huxley in his exclusion of God's causal activity. His purpose is ultimately the naturalistic ethical one of laying it down that "man must cease being afraid of his uniqueness, and must not continue to put off the responsibilities that are really his on to the shoulders of mythical gods or meta-physical absolutes." [49] On the positive side, Huxley seeks to establish a conjunction between the forces at work in the development of the inorganic universe and those in the living world. He speaks in a comprehensive way about a three-stage evolution from the nonliving to the living and to the human, but he does not make a detailed analysis of the common causal meaning underlying force in the physical system, biological agency, and cultural power.

As Huxley uses the term, "mechanical" serves mainly the negative function of removing any purpose or intelligent guidance from the development of biological species. He stresses that the causal principles of evolution are blind and purposeless, without going into any further detail about the positive way in which evolutionary agencies are related to the mechanical principles in a system of physical change. Once he has eliminated the possibility of teleology as implying an intelligent agent distinct from nature, Huxley is quite gener-

---

[49] J. Huxley, *Evolution: the Modern Synthesis* (New York: Harper, 1942), p. 578.

ous in what he ascribes to evolutionary workings. They issue in real adaptations, apart from any purposive intending by a mind. In the Huxleyan universe, there are adaptations without purposes, final results without finality, directions without intelligent directing. And he intends this contrast to hold good in the real order in an unconditioned way, rather than to signify merely a methodological limitation placed upon the biological procedures.

As far as biologists are concerned, the creative and mechanical character of the evolutionary mechanism *can* be taken in a methodological sense which does not necessarily commit them to Huxley's metaphysical standpoint. But it is more difficult for them to give a similar purely procedural meaning to his third note of "progressiveness" and hence it is the most controversial one for them. He explains carefully that evolutionary progress is neither necessary nor universal and that it is not identical with all the results of natural selection.[50] It requires considerable selection of evidence and construction of a conceptual model before the meaning of a progressive evolutionary mechanism can be established. Despite the many instances of degeneration and stagnant equilibrium, there is the fact of dominant types appearing at various eras as improvements of living stocks. The criteria for determining such dominant types are their greater control over the changing environment and their increasing independence of action. Through these traits they attain a broader biological efficiency than do other forms and thus they represent an evolutionary progress.

At this point, Huxley makes the transition from pre-human evolution to that of man.[51] Man is continuous with organic nature, since the same causal agencies of selection and mutation operate in producing the human organism. But Huxley also insists on man's unique-

---

[50] On the biological basis for the concept of evolutionary progress, see *Evolution: the Modern Synthesis*, pp. 556–69, and J. Huxley, *Evolution in Action* (New York: Harper, 1953), pp. 124–51.

[51] *Ibid.*, pp. 152–76; *Evolution: the Modern Synthesis*, pp. 570–78; *Evolution as a Process*, pp. 11–13. Huxley adopts a Bergsonian accent in holding that "the evolutionary process, as now embodied in man, has for the first time become aware of itself, is studying the laws of its own unfolding."—*Evolution as a Process*, p. 13.

ness in respect to his particular genesis, his present mode of being, and especially his prospects for the future. Only the evolutionary line which actually did give rise to man could have done so, since it was the only one that could give rise to a form of life which is capable of true speech and conceptual thought. These are distinctive features of man's present mode of being, and on this score Huxley resists any efforts to whittle them down by comparative analysis or genetic psychology.

His chief reason for the nonreductive view of man's present capacities is to give evolutionary humanism a program and a hope for the future. Quite literally, he sees no future possibility of evolutionary progress except through man's agency. All other lines of descent have lead into blind alleys, but man alone has found a substitute for genetic mutation. His intelligence permits him to transform biological into cultural progress, since he can retain, criticize, and heighten his social and individual experience. At the human level, then, progress must include not only the objective notes of biological efficiency but also some subjective notes of human value. Like Comte, Huxley adds a subjective criterion to the objective one as soon as he comes to the human plane and turns his face to the future outlook.

Now it becomes clear why Huxley insisted on giving an ontological and antitheistic meaning to the general description of the evolutionary mechanism. His long-range aim was so to describe these general factors that they would furnish a causal pattern of a definite sort to serve as an objective basis and norm for human choice. God was ruled out not because of the biological facts and concepts but because of the desire to anticipate the question of human valuational choice, which must not be governed by any extranatural considerations. It was not Huxley the ornithologist and biological synthesizer but Huxley the naturalistic philosopher who specified the antitheistic meaning for the creative and mechanical aspects of the evolutionary agency. His naturalistic humanism is not merely continuous with his scientific views on evolution but transforms them into stages of a philosophical argument.

The criteria of evolutionary progress—control, independence, capacity for advance and, at the human level, capacity for increased experience—become the criteria for ethical action and religiousness, once we come to reflect on them and generalize them as the sole guides for human decision. By responding deeply to the task of advancing the evolutionary line in terms of intensified human experience of individuals and social groups, we can enjoy all the values of moral and religious experience without calling upon any absolute. The standards of ethical choice are relative to the given stage of the evolutionary process, but they also have a certain permanence as long as the human type persists and can reflect on this process. "The ultimate guarantees for the correctness of our labels of rightness and wrongness are to be sought for among the facts of evolutionary direction." [52] This is the decisive sense in which Huxley's philosophical preoccupations tend to transform all of his scientific descriptions of evolutionary mechanism and its general notes. He makes them furnish a basis for restricting humanistic religion to a feeling of awe and a practical commitment to the evolutionary forces immanent in nature, the individual self, and society. Hence although Huxley agrees explicitly with Father Teilhard de Chardin on our obligation to promote convergent cooperation among men rather than divergent competition, he denies that any future phase of evolutionary transcendence can lead men to the presence of God.

Huxley's evolutionary humanism has become the focal point for some interesting critical discussion of evolutionism from various standpoints. The geneticist Theodosius Dobzhansky is skeptical about drawing our ethical criteria from his science: The evolutionary and the eternal perspectives on human life are distinct and unreducible one to the other. He presents two objections against making an ethical use of evolutionary findings. On the factual side, there

[52] This statement concludes Julian Huxley's own Romanes Lecture on "Evolutionary Ethics," in T. H. Huxley and J. Huxley, *Touchstone for Ethics*, p. 156; cf. pp. 199, 228. Julian Huxley presents his synthesis of atheistic naturalism and a religious attitude in *Religion without Revelation* (revised ed., New York: Harper, 1957). Of special interest is his personal confession (pp. 65–96) of combining a highly religious response to nature with only the most casual acquaintance with any intellectual evidence for theism. Cuénot, *L'évolution biologique*, pp. 568–69, sees little difference between a pantheistic and a naturalistic approach to nature in religious terms.

are many trends at work within the several species, including man.
To define *the* direction of evolution as the one which promotes the
traits which Huxley regards as progressive depends upon making a
selection among actual tendencies and then defining directionality of
evolution in these terms. This is not only a highly selective and constructural procedure but also leads to the second point of showing
why we ought to take our duty from the results of such selection.
Given man's freedom, he can call evolutionary directional progress
into question as a norm for his choice. Merely the repetition that
this is the constructed meaning for progress does not answer the question of why we should be obliged morally to take the progressive
path at all. The question cannot be stilled by a form of cosmic
intimidation about how the forces in the world are moving, since we
make our moral choices on distinctively human grounds and not simply on descriptive translations of the prevailing forces in biological
evolution. "Human acts and aspirations may be morally right or
morally wrong, regardless of whether they assist the evolutionary
process to proceed in the direction in which it has been going, or
whether they assist it in any direction at all." [53] Evolutionary considerations are sometimes too vague and sometimes simply irrelevant to the task of determining our moral obligation and ordering of
values in the concrete situation of moral choice.

The zoologist Paul Moody concludes his recent study of evolution
with a personal acceptance of God as the source of natural laws of
life and the goal of evolutionary process. Looking at all the blind
alleys, retrogressions, and random actions involved in the course of
evolution, he asks: "May not they in themselves form part of the pattern? Why should we assume that the laws of the universe, including those of evolution, must be so organized as to reach a goal by
what seems to our human minds the most direct route?" [54] His point
is not that there is no pattern or route to discern, but that it has to

---

[53] T. Dobzhansky, *The Biological Basis of Human Freedom* (New York:
Columbia University Press, 1956), p. 131.

[54] P. A. Moody, *Introduction to Evolution* (New York: Harper, 1953), p.
432. A similar point is made philosophically by C. A. Hartshorne, "Outlines
of a Philosophy of Nature. Part II," *The Personalist*, XXXIX (1958), 385–89,
with a use of Peirce's logic of chance against Huxley's anti-finalism.

be studied comprehensively in its own actual contours rather than measured abstractly and selectively by some particular conception of economy of mechanical action. As Peirce noted, there is a logical pattern for the interplay of chance and law and for the gradual growth of the latter under conditions of contingency. God's purposive intelligence can achieve the gradual emergence of a many-leveled cosmos through this evolutionary polarity, rendering questionable the divorcement which Huxley proposes between adaptation and purpose, selective progress and a theistic context for the whole account of evolution.

Philosophers of science have started to study the trend among Neo-Darwinians to erase the distinction between a descriptive and a causally explanatory concept. Marjorie Grene suggests that correlations based on statistical trends in population groups do not themselves constitute, and only indirectly indicate, some of the real causal factors present in living nature. Hence such data do not justify the philosophical inference drawn by Huxley and his American colleague, George Simpson, that the selective-genetic mechanism is the total and exclusive cause of the biological changes observed in evolutionary process. What we today refer to as the selective-genetic mechanism is a complex concept, containing a direct element of causal agency in generation along with some considerable interpretation of population facts by the inquiring mind. This combination of real causal factors and descriptive instruments of probable explanation cannot be regarded as a massive flow of uniform causal power, and still less can it be appealed to philosophically as being simply the biological expression of an all-sufficient causal principle of cosmic evolution. When genetical selection is treated in a descriptive way as a tool of explanation bearing some reference to causal agency but not simply equated with a purposeless mechanical cause, it loses none of its mathematical rigor or its biological usefulness in developing the explanations proper to this discipline. It only ceases to support Simpson's and Huxley's philosophical exclusion of God as the ultimate intelligent cause and goal of nature. We can expect that genetics will follow the example of quantum physics in reflecting upon the meaning and limitations of its causal language, without regarding physical types of explanation as its own model.

Grene admits that if the meaning of the term "scientific" is confined to the mechanical prototype, then the Neo-Darwinian stress upon the genetic-selective mechanism has the advantage of being logically simple and automatic. But in addition to logical simplicity and automatism, every evolutionary theory must also be measured by its adequacy in admitting all the factors which are required in our actual explanatory efforts. In this respect, the Huxley position proves to be reductionist and hence to be lacking in explanatory range.

Where concepts of more than one logical level are necessary to the interpretation of a set of phenomena, we ought not to pretend to be operating on one level only. In the context of evolution where we in fact acknowledge novel operational principles, we should not pretend that nothing is there but the conditions without which (admittedly) they could not operate. The sum total of necessary conditions for the coming into being of an individual, a species, a phylum or of life itself are not logically or historically identical *with* the individual, or species, or phylum, or life itself. . . . I suggest, therefore, that instead of Ockham's razor we might adopt as a test of theories of evolution the opposite principle: that entities, or more generally perhaps aspects of reality—for principles of organization are not entities, though they do define entities—should not be *subtracted* beyond what is honest.[55]

This inverse criterion is specially pertinent when it is a question of transmuting present biological theory into philosophical evolutionism as a naturalistic account of the genesis of the universe.

In his analytic study of the philosophical uses of scientific thinking, Stephen Toulmin uses Huxley's evolutionary naturalism as a case history in the transition from scientific explanation to scientifically oriented myth. The passage is made whenever a selected biological order is treated as the Sovereign Order of Nature and thus proposed as the ethical norm for men. In the past, the Aristotelian

[55] M. Grene, "Two Evolutionary Theories," *The British Journal for the Philosophy of Science,* IX (1958), 192, 193. In "The Influence of Evolutionary Theory upon American Thought," *Gregorianum,* XXXII (1951), 582-90, G. P. Klubertanz, S.J., shows the difference between describing some lines of descent and furnishing a total causal explanation.

scale of nature was so used, and at present the evolutionary tree of life is serving the same purpose. The mythic use of evolution by Spencer was noted long ago by Chauncey Wright. For his part, Toulmin specifies two criteria for recognizing when a scientific concept is being mythologized.[56] The concept must be used in an extended sense rather than in its straight scientific meaning, and the extension must be made for motives other than the explanatory aims of the science in question. When these conditions are fulfilled, disputes that may arise in regard to the full-blown myth cannot be settled by having recourse to the usual scientific procedures, even though the myth itself may continue to thrive upon the achievements of the scientific substrate.

Huxley's appeal to evolutionary progress as an ethical and religious principle displays these two traits. In his usage, "evolution" is the evocative term for a highly selective and complex conceptual artefact. Biological selection is linked up vaguely at one end with physico-chemical events in the inorganic world, and at the other end it is made continuous with the moral and religious aims of human society. The resulting cosmic image includes far more than the theory of natural selection and genetic mutation, so that critical discussion of its scope and use cannot reach a conclusion by reference to the data and procedures in biology. Evolutionary process now assumes the mythic status of the Sovereign Order of Nature and, as such, provides a standard and sanction for our moral choices and religious aspirations. Huxley's complex constructural account of evolution is intended not as a testable scientific hypothesis but rather as a stabilizing, controlling, and consoling image of the world for the use of naturalistic humanists. As distinct from the scientific notion of evolution based on genetics and paleontology, this evolutionary myth functions as a means of securing cosmic backing for the transition from *is* to *ought*, from impersonal survival-value of the stock to convergent value as the moral good and duty of man. To use Dewey's

[56] S. Toulmin, "Contemporary Scientific Mythology," *Metaphysical Beliefs*, by S. Toulmin, R. W. Hepburn, and A. MacIntyre (London: SCM Press, 1957), pp. 50–65.

language, the mythic imagery of evolution serves to underwrite the naturalistic version of the quest for certainty in human values.

In his major treatise on *The Sources of Value,* S. C. Pepper reopens the question of the ethical significance of survival value and its relation to the rest of the human value system. He criticizes the tooth-and-claw version of survival, since modern biological research brings out the importance of cooperation and interdependence of the various species and their individual members. He also rejects Julian Huxley's notion of continuous evolutionary progress as the norm for determining ethical values and obligations. Pepper observes that on this score Huxley does not enjoy the full support of Simpson and other leading evolutionists. We can discover various modes of adaptation within some definite zone of life and then determine the dominant form within that situation. But there are many zones of life, some of them unrelated in time and biological competition and some of them existing contemporaneously and yet with little or no competition. We cannot significantly grade as lower and higher the dominant forms in these different life zones, since their dominance refers to their mode of adaptation within their own life situation and not to a succession of forms passing from one such zone to another. There is no continuous march of evolutionary progress from one dominant form to another, culminating at last in man.

In short, there are as many dynamically sanctioned lines of biological progress as there are life zones within which adaptation is going on through natural selection. But there is no dynamically sanctioned line of progress across life zones, and consequently none for the course of evolutionary history as a whole.[57]

Hence a carefully constructed evolutionary theory will not attempt to provide a cosmic sanction for the features which have enabled man to survive, and will not erect them into a value standard on the basis of their being identical with some universal norm of evolutionary progress.

[57] S. C. Pepper, *The Sources of Value* (Berkeley and Los Angeles: University of California Press, 1958), p. 625. Pepper restates his case succinctly in his *Ethics* (New York: Appleton-Century-Crofts, 1960), pp. 199–223, but does not clarify the naturalistic basis of obligation.

Pepper's critique is significant on several counts. For one thing, it suggests that the relation between evolutionary theory and the notion of cosmic progress is just as problematic today as in the time of Spencer. Hence it counsels the ethician and value philosopher against taking the easy road of invoking progress as a basis for moral judgments. A second point is that Pepper returns to a position much closer to that of Darwin himself, both in stressing the plural lines of evolutionary adaptation and in looking for the value significance of survival directly in the operation of natural selection in human life, rather than in any essential link between natural selection and some schema of progress. He also credits Darwin with seeing that the precise way in which natural selection operates most effectively in the region of man is through his intelligence and moral conscience. Cultural evolution is not discontinuous with biological evolution, since they are both present in human development and both furnish modes of operation for securing the survival of the human species. Pepper does not reduce purposive values simply to that of survival, but he does maintain that in any situation of ultimate decision the latter must be dominant. His conclusion is that natural selection in its cultural and social form is the ultimate sanction for all human values and obligations. Where he differs from Huxley is in taking the selective process as an ultimate evaluative process in itself, without need for any further sanction in a structure of continuous cosmic progress.

7. Conclusion

The outcome of this study of the impact of Darwin and evolutionary theories upon philosophy can be briefly stated. Perhaps the most striking point is the variety of philosophic responses that have been evoked by the evolutionary findings in biology. The scientific data and theories do not necessarily generate by their own weight any one single conclusion in the philosophical order or support one favored general interpretation of the universe. This is where an analysis of the consequences of evolution for philosophy proper must be carefully distinguished from a psychological and cultural description in terms of the history of ideas. The latter approach is valuable for underlining certain pervasive concrete traits in our contemporary outlook which are either derived from evolutionary thought or greatly strengthened by it. For instance, we are now accustomed to a vastly enlarged time scale and to a view of time itself as a struggling, creative, irreversible process bringing forth ever novel forms of life. We take a genetic and historical approach to everything, looking for the meaning and the possibilities of things in their path of growth and the seed of novelty they contain. Man's kinship with the organic world is recognized, his thoroughly temporal and historical mode of reality is being explored, and the feeling is abroad that he stands at the threshold of a new mode of life. These convictions belong to our evolutionary atmosphere as a matter of daily respiration. Nevertheless, they remain fundamentally neutral as far as the major philosophical issues are concerned. The common stock of evolutionary ideas is open to diverse and conflicting philosophical interpretations. The idealist and the naturalist, the phenomenologist and the realistic theist, are all fully aware of the descriptive notes in the evolutionary climate, but the cultural facts themselves are not decisive for settling the principal differences among these philosophers.

This does not mean that evolutionary research is irrelevant for philosophy but only that its contribution has to be estimated in every instance through the proper canons of philosophical inquiry and cannot be automatically registered. We have seen this to be the case in the two problems of physico-theology and progress. A careful historical description and philosophical evaluation are required to determine the precise grounds of conflict between the Derham-Paley argument from design and the biological position of Darwin. A further analysis is needed to find out whether or not the untenability of Paley's watch argument entails the abandoning of all natural theology and hence leads to agnosticism as an unavoidable standpoint. Again, the question of whether there is any sort of progress in the universe and human history is not completely decided on biological and physical grounds, although they may rule out certain lines of argument or show that other views are more likely. There is still the problem of whether a philosophical conception can be found to account for random, retrogressive, and cyclic instances.

Among philosophers of evolution, the persistent problem has been that of making the transition from the scientific data and hypotheses about evolution to a philosophical evolutionism. This is a question of methodology which does not get resolved simply by watching what the scientific contributors to evolutionary theory do. For many of them do not enlarge their work to include a philosophical signifi- cance, and those who do follow this path are employing some addi- tional instruments of philosophical generalization which are precisely what still require analysis and evaluation. We have noticed some divergent ways in which men conceive the right method for gen- eralizing evolutionary thought. Wright claims that there is no specu- latively valid method available; Peirce looks for it in a logic of the growth of law or reasonableness; Dewey finds it in converting the scientific mode of description into a naturalistic logic and ontology; Harris appeals to the idealistic notion of immanent mind; Bergson plunges into interior awareness of temporal duration.

One useful result of taking a synoptic historical view of these posi- tions is that it furnishes a strong reminder of the persistent difficul- ties surrounding evolutionism as a philosophical claim. Anyone sharing the climate of evolution in its scientific and cultural aspects finds it difficult to retain a vivid sense of the problematic character of evolutionary discussion when it begins to supply general answers about the origin of the universe, the nature of causal relations and what they exclude, and the basis of moral obligation and religious search. Yet it is illusory to think that one can move continuously and without any further instruments from genetics and paleontology into these other areas. The value of a critically used methodology is to dispel this illusion by distinguishing the scientific aspects of evo- lution from philosophical evolutionism and requiring the latter to face explicitly the task of reflecting upon and testing the bases in method and evidence for a generalized interpretation of evolution.

To recognize a mythic element in much contemporary speculation on evolution is not to pass any judgment on the intrinsic soundness of that speculation. It is intended only to clarify from another perspective the point that the incorporation of scientific findings and theories about evolution into a general view of the universe and human destiny requires more justification than a loose restatement of the scientific findings and theories themselves. Largely under the pressure of the evolutionary mode of thinking in all fields, we have lost confidence in the Newtonian model of the world machine and yet have not been able to live familiarly with any of the newer physical accounts, some of which discourage any efforts at visualization of the mathematical theory. Yet men insistently require some concrete symbols and analogies expressing the significance of the universe and human history to them. And since in a scientific age this demand gets focused upon the resources of the sciences, the tendency is to build the imagery from a basis in the more concrete evolutionary sciences. Thus one of the cultural functions of evolutionary speculation today is to grope toward a humanly satisfying, as well as approximately correct, image of the developing universe and man's role in it.

The functions of philosophy, however, are never exhaustively described in terms of present cultural needs. Philosophy is here to make us critically aware of both the validity and the limitations of the evidence, the complex reference of scientific theories to the natural world as well as to the mind's constructural operations, and the mythic fusion on the side of the human subject, all of which are cooperating in trying to provide an evolutionary image for our age. Because of its deliberately critical and reflective standpoint, philosophy cannot merely submit to the impact of evolutionary thought and serve as a component in the process of forming an evolutionary outlook. It must continue to assess, restrict, and revise this process, as well as hold before our view other ways of looking at the world and forming our patterns of conduct. Philosophies which remain loyal to their methodological and critical tasks are never fully integrated with the reigning world-image, evolutionary or otherwise, but retain a certain salutary distance which keeps us responsive to the rigorous demands of inquiry and always open to new ways of reaching evidence.

The need to make a personal appraisal of the scientific sources on evolution stands out plainly in a comparison between Julian Huxley and Father Pierre Teilhard de Chardin, S.J. Teilhard's work is becoming increasingly known to scientists and theologians, but as yet it has not influenced the philosophers of evolution very deeply.[58] Both Huxley and Teilhard are working from roughly the same evidence, although the latter stresses his own field of paleontology and human development. Each approaches the task of finding the general significance of evolution not only with the resources of his scientific training but also with those of his philosophy and his faith—faith in self-contained nature in the one instance and faith in the revealing God in the other. They agree upon the convergent and cooperative character of evolutionary forces at the human level, as well as that man embodies a distinctive living reality, what Teilhard calls the noösphere within the encompassing biosphere. Furthermore, both inquirers maintain that present-day man is not the final stage in the evolutionary process but that still higher modes of living lie open for realization by human social agencies.

Yet they disagree sharply about the kind of reality which lies beyond the evolutionary threshold or "point omega" toward which human history is moving. For Huxley, this next level can be characterized at least negatively as involving no reality which transcends the totality of evolving nature itself. Teilhard, on the other hand, describes the evolutionary convergence as leading man into the presence of God as the personal, energic source of all life, immanent in and also personally distinct from natural process. Thus Teilhard arrives at a spiritual and theistic conception of evolution. But he

[58] A brief sketch is made in English by A. Knodel, "An Introduction to the Integral Evolutionism of Teilhard de Chardin," *The Personalist*, XXXVIII (1957), 347–55. Longer studies have been written by C. Tresmontant, *Pierre Teilhard de Chardin: His Thought* (Baltimore: Helicon Press, 1959), and by Claude Cuénot, *Pierre Teilhard de Chardin: Les grandes étapes de son évolution* (Paris: Plon, 1958). A bibliography of writings by and on Teilhard was compiled by Leo Larkin, S.J., for *Woodstock College Library Chapbook I*, April 1958, pp. 7–15.

does so with the aid of some arguments which at least implicitly are philosophical in significance.

In terms of the present survey, we can orient Teilhard's position with respect to some of the main philosophical tendencies. He agrees with the idealists, especially Harris and personalism, that we should reinterpret the emergence of mind from matter in a finalistic way. It does not mean that mind is reducible to its organic basis but rather that "spirit is cosmically more important than matter, more valuable, more powerful, more final." [59] Thus a teleological approach can be taken, in which the emergence of spirit is a token of its unique reality and dominating importance. Yet Teilhard does not lessen the naturalistic insistence that the emergence of a new level of reality with man required a slight organic transformation. The point is that by means of this organic change there is introduced into the universe a new factor, so that it is now possible to reflect upon the nature of evolution and to control its future course.

On the methodological issue of finding in man's distinctive con-

---

[59] This and the following quotation are from Pierre Teilhard de Chardin, S.J., "Spiritualistic Evolution," *ibid.*, pp. 17, 18. Two brief statements of some philosophical and theological issues raised by evolution, especially as it applies to man, are made by L. Dufault, O.M.I., "The Philosophical and Biological Implications of Evolution," *Proceedings of the American Catholic Philosophical Association*, XXVI (1952), 66–80, and by C. Vollert, S.J., "Evolution of the Human Body," *The Catholic Mind*, L (1952), 135–54. Recent theological interest in time and history should avoid two pitfalls. One is the confusion sometimes made between a rigorously cyclic theory of cosmic change and the spiral sort of advance envisioned by Vico and Teilhard. The other danger is that of over-simplifying the problem of the roots of contemporary concern for time and history to the point where all positive conceptions are treated merely as a secularizing and mythologizing of the Christian outlook. Although evolutionary thought is much more ambiguous about historical progress than is usually recognized, this does not lessen the fact that some aspects of evolutionism do furnish an irreducible source of our present awareness of time and history which is not just a transposition of theological themes. In one of his last essays, in *L'apparition de l'homme* (Paris: Éditions du Seuil, 1956), pp. 335–74, Teilhard stresses the evolutionary intimacy of God's causal operation and argues (against Huxley and Simpson) that the hominization of the world must give birth not only to a deepened sense of the historical but also to our reflective union with the transcendent God. Huxley states both an appreciation and a criticism of Teilhard's position in his Introduction to *The Phenomenon of Man* (New York: Harper, 1959), which is the first of Teilhard de Chardin's major books to be translated into English.

sciousness a means of access to the general nature and finalizing import of evolutionary process, Teilhard remains close to Bergson and even to Huxley. "If man is nothing else than evolution become conscious of itself, man, then, in order to be true to himself and to the universe, has to push forward individually and socially, the spiritual progress of nature." The reality of progress and the irreversibility of the growth toward spiritual reality are not left ambiguous by Teilhard, who accepts them at the same time that he rejects any facile optimism about automatic improvement. We have to work hard as persons and social groups to maintain human existence and achieve any advance. By contrast with naturalistic humanism, however, Teilhard combines a stress upon man's natural origin and transforming capacities with a wholehearted religious acceptance of God. Ours is a gradually awakening universe, and what we are awakening to is the common summons of all forms of life and especially man's spiritual reality to a convergent sharing in the life of the personal God. Thus for post-Darwinian man, the meaning of mechanism is transformed to integrate it with teleology and the effective presence of God in the course of evolutionary striving.

In the deadlock between Huxley and Teilhard over an ultimate interpretation of evolution, we can observe how the scientific sources of evidence do not entirely determine the structure of an evolutionary philosophy. Especially in the case of the persistent problem of the relation between descriptive and causal elements in our concept of the agencies in evolutionary change, a broadened and reflective philosophical analysis of the scientific findings and language is unavoidable. Even when the contribution of the various components is discriminated, there remains the further issue of how biological causation is related to a cosmic evolutionary process, and whether the evolutionary causal explanations are the only ones required to account for our universe in causal terms. Thus the questions of *generalization and causality* in evolutionary theory tend to make a juncture, indicating for the philosopher that they constitute the core of any present-day study of evolutionism.

The philosopher's duty is to make a careful scrutiny of all the contributing factors in our contemporary evolutionary outlooks. This involves a study of the natural world of real organisms and their processes, the scientific constructs and theories, the controlling world-imagery, the naturalistic or theistic working faiths, and the philosophical methods and concepts being used. In addition, however, the philosophical inquirer must bring to bear some other human resources which may not figure immediately as components in some prevailing evolutionary position. He has to consult what is suggested about the nature of temporal process and history, the structure of human experience and the ways to God, by philosophies not so directly implicated in the biological work of Darwin and his successors as are the philosophical positions considered here. This is a complex task. But to become aware of the need for it and of the futility of expecting any pre-packaged solution of evolutionary difficulties is the first step toward getting it done. In the problem of evolution as well as everywhere else in the philosophy of nature, our philosophical judgment rests ultimately upon our personal study and evaluation of the whole tissue of relevant sources open to men.

A NOTE ON THEOLOGY AND EVOLUTION

ROBERT W. GLEASON

The controversies over evolution that excited the nineteenth century and the beginning of the twentieth century have to a certain extent disappeared from theological literature. While the origin of man and the question of his parents will always be a matter of vital interest, present-day theologians are far more moderate in their claims than were their predecessors. Similarly, modern scientists seem to be more content to remain within the area of their respective fields with their appropriate probabilities and certitudes than were some of their forerunners.[1] At one time in theology a certain funda-

---

[1] For a balanced evaluation in English of both anthropological and theological data on human evolution, F. Ewing's "Human Evolution—1956," *Anthropological Quarterly*, Oct., 1956, pp. 91–139, should be consulted. In addition to this and to the other works cited in the notes to the present study, the following publications may prove helpful to further study of the theological implications of evolution: F. Ceuppens, *Genèse I–III* (Paris: Desclée, 1945); *Gregorianum*, XXIX (1948), 342–527 (a symposium); A. M. Henry, *God and His Creation* (Chicago: Fides, 1955); A. Jones, *Unless Some Man Show Me* (New York: Sheed and Ward, 1957); V. Marcozzi, *Evoluzione o creazione* (Milan, 1948); P. M. Perier, *Le transformisme, l'origine de l'homme et le dogme catholique* (Paris: Beauchesne, 1938); B. de Solanges, "Christianity and Evolution," *Cross Currents*, I (1951), 26–37; T. Steinbuchel, *Die Abstammung des Menschen* (Frankfurt, 1951); B. Vawter, *A Path Through Genesis* (New York: Sheed and Ward, 1957); C. Vollert, "Human Evolution and Theological Implications," *Proceedings, American Catholic Theological Society*, 1951, pp. 122–45.

mentalism seemed to be popular. What is known today as concord-
ism, that is, the effort to treat the Bible as though its apparently
literal expressions were teaching facts of science, no longer finds
favor with exegetes or theologians.[2] Nonetheless, the teaching body
of the Church, the official *magisterium*, still exercises vigilance over
the writings of theologians where these touch the origins of man and
especially his derivation from a single pair.

It is evident today that the Sacred Books of other Semitic cultures,
the Egyptian, the Sumerian, the Assyrian, bear remarkable similarity
to the Bible in many details, while they are wholly different in the
affirmations they conceal beneath their imagery. Today we realize
that theological opportunism is of very little apologetic value. Moreover, exegetes are willing to recognize certain facets of biblical interpretation which seemed foreign to nineteenth-century thought.
In the first chapter of Genesis, the section which causes most problems for the theologian interested in evolution, there are undoubtedly images, expressions and elements of popular folklore common to
other cultures besides that of the Israelites. It is no longer popular to
consider all these elements as having been dictated by God.[3] Again,
there are two different accounts of the creation of man in this chapter
of Genesis and the author of the first account is evidently a very different personality from the author of the second. While all theologians agree that history is expressed in the assertions of Genesis,
nevertheless today they admit that it is a peculiar type of history
whose rules are still partly unknown to us. There are certain definite
ways to telling a story, certain idioms which are peculiar to the
Semitic language and which do not correspond to any of our categories of Greco-Roman history or of modern literary forms. Modern
archaeological research is enabling us to come much closer to the
original meaning of Genesis and in doing so, some of the barriers to
a modern form of evolution are being removed for the theologian.[4]

[2] Cf. E. Arbez, "Genesis I–XI and Prehistory," *American Ecclesiastical Review*, CXXIII (1950), 82–83. Cf. *ibid.*, pp. 86–87.
[3] Cf. C. Hauret, *Beginnings; Genesis and Modern Science* (Dubuque: Priory
Press, 1955), p. 16.
[4] Ewing, "Human Evolution—1956," *Anthrop. Qtrly.*, Oct., 1956, pp. 123–27.

The first narrative of the creation and especially of the account of the creation of man probably does not go back to the actual date of Moses, that is, to the thirteenth or the fifteenth century before Christ but is rather a sort of theological résumé of Mosaic tradition. It is a popular account of the creation of man, adapted to the memory of the oriental people and yet, it is not popular in the sense that it is as imaged as the second creation account. To understand this we must realize that the human author whom God chooses as an instrument of His message works within the secular framework of his own time. He shares the so-called scientific notions of his contemporaries based upon personal observation and experience. The sacred author communicates a divine thought to us, through the medium of scientific notions which are a part of the mental culture of his own time. He is, after all, attempting to express things in terms in which his readers can understand him. It is possible that the scientific notions of the author of Genesis are erroneous, drawn as they are from contemporary science but it is not these notions that he is affirming or implying. It is not the intention of Sacred Scripture to teach us cosmogony. It preserves neutrality before various hypotheses concerning the original development of life and mankind in this world.

With regard to the question of the evolution of the human body, the problem which most intrigues Catholic scholars, the air has been considerably cleared since the nineteenth century.[5] Numerous Catholic scholars are prepared today to admit a form of theistic transformism or evolution. Exegetes and theologians are today more concerned with observing the demands which theology places upon itself as a science and with pointing out the demands which scientific evolutionary theories should place upon themselves as sciences. The origin of the human body by way of evolution does not appear improbable today. Many anthropologists believe that there is some genetic and physical connection between man and lower animals. This is at least a working hypothesis which the theologian must treat

---

Cf. E. Boné, "L'homme: genèse et cheminement," *Nouvelle Revue Théologique*, 1947, p. 389.
    [5] Cf. Achille Cardinal Liénart, "Science and the Bible," *The Commonweal*, June 24, 1949, pp. 265–67.

as such, and within the framework of his own science determine how much validity can be granted to it.[6] Although Scripture says that God formed Adam from the dust of the earth, it may well be that the dust refers rather to organic matter oriented by God through a long process. We no longer feel it necessary to hold that God formed the body of man immediately and directly from inorganic matter. It is true that some years ago many theologians viewed such trans-formism with anything but favor, since transformism was so frequently anti-theistic in its implications and connected with many other theories scarcely calculated to please Catholic thinkers. The conclusions of scientists which are debatable should be controlled by their own science and conclusions of theology should also be controlled by its scientific methods. The certain should be distinguished from the probable and the possible, and the unchanging affirmations of Scriptures should be distinguished from the interpretations of exegetes and from the images used by the first writer. From the first creation account we can derive the fact that man owes his existence to a special intervention on the part of God. But we are unable to decide with certainty *from the text* when this intervention of God took place, whether it took place upon organic or inorganic matter and how many human beings were in question. It is not easy either to decide *from the text* of the first creation account whether Adam and Eve were a single couple or many primitive couples.[7]

The second account clarifies many of the questions which were left unclear from the first account. In the first account the author told of the origin of the universe in terms of a science of his day, and in the second account the author pictured the creation of man according to his own ideas of what man is. The second account portrays a Creator molding clay as a potter and breathing life into it. These are images that were traditional to Israelite culture, and in fact, in other texts of Babylonian literature we see similar stories recounted. Egyptian

---

[6] Cf. W. Hauber, "Evolution and Catholic Thought," *American Ecclesiastical Review*, CVI (1942), 161–64.

[7] Cf. P. Chaine, *Le Livre de la Genèse* (Paris: Cerf, 1948), p. 46; also M. Gruenthaner, "Evolution and the Scriptures," *Catholic Biblical Quarterly*, XIII (1951), 21–27, for the scriptural evidence against polygenism.

folklore has its god Khnum who created man, modeling him upon a potter's wheel. Other folklores tell us of goddesses modeling men and women from clay. What the sacred author is insisting upon is the fact that at the origin of man, the creator God is seen and that He stands at the origin of both man's body and soul. Man is the master of his own destiny and, gifted with intelligence and will, he resembles God Himself. There is a very special poetic setting set forth by the author in order to show us that man and only man caused God to intervene in a special fashion in his creation.[8]

The nature of the divine intervention in the formation of Adam's body is not entirely clear. We know that man is a being endowed with freedom of choice and intellectual processes and as such must have an immaterial soul directly created by God. Is it possible that the divine intervention consisted merely in the vivification by an immortal soul of previously organically organized matter? That the human soul is due to a special intervention of God in the form of creation is irreversible Catholic teaching. As a spiritual substance, this human soul comes directly from the hands of God who creates it in each individual case. Is it possible that the sacred author is simply expressing this reality of the joining of the spiritual soul to organic matter by his image of God breathing into matter? In order to obtain some kind of a picture of the divine intervention by which the human body was formed, we do not have to resort to the primitive ideas condemned by Augustine which envision God molding earth to the form of a human body and then breathing into that earth a human soul.

It is perfectly acceptable to maintain that God created man's body directly from inorganic matter and by an act of his will caused that matter to be animated by the spiritual soul. However, some modern theologians, approaching the text with much more knowledge of paleontological discoveries, feel that it is also possible to interpret the text as saying that God drew the human body from an animal organism which was transformed so as to receive a human soul. It

[8] Hauret, op. cit., p. 94. Cf. Gruenthaner, "Evolution . . . ," Cath. Bib. Qtrly., XIII (1951), 24–26, on the nature of the intervention.

is possible that this transformation occurred before the infusion of the human soul, so that God retouched, as it were, an animal organism and the animal became a living person upon the infusion of the divinely created soul. Thus the body of man may actually have been enjoying some animal or subhuman life when God infused the spiritual soul into it. If we accept the fact that the human came into being at the end of a series of sudden mutations directed to this end by the Creator God, then these changes reveal God's Providence throughout. At a certain point, the animal organism in question may have been sufficiently perfected so that it was ready for the last touches preceding the infusion of the human soul. But we must not conceive this perfection as though it *required* the infusion of a human soul from purely immanent intramundane processes. Rather, the mutations which prepared for the soul would be directed by God and His special action throughout.

Whatever theory one holds, one must always accept the fact that the creation of man is peculiar in several senses. The creation of his soul is due directly to the creative act of God, and his body itself is formed by a peculiar intervention of the Most High. Whether this intervention consists in the transformation of purely inorganic matter, or in a divine alteration of an animal organism, or in the elevation of subhuman activities in order to prepare and dispose for the reception of the soul, we must in any event maintain that the man Adam arose, *body and soul*, from a special intervention on the part of God. By reason of his intellectual nature, man is directly related to his Creator and requires this intervention of God, which is expressed in the text by the act of God breathing life into him. Whether this be reorganization of a pre-existing animal organism, whether it be the transformation of the dust of the earth in a literal sense, or whether it be by the infusion of the human soul, the sacred text does not explicitly say. However, we can be sure that the hypotheses of the purely animal origin of man is excluded. Man is in no sense a child of an animal.[9] Pius XII in the encyclical *Humani Generis* has said that the Church does not forbid research and discussion by men

[9] M. Flick. "L'Origine del corpo del primo uomo," *Gregorianum,* 1948, p. 366.

of theology and science with regard to the doctrine of evolution in so far as this doctrine inquires into the origin of the human body as coming from pre-existing living matter. But the Catholic Faith obliges us to hold that all human souls are immediately created by God. With modesty and moderation the expert may submit his reasons on one side or the other with regard to mitigated, theistic transformism.

We cannot accept the theory that the transformation from one species to another took place as a result of causes purely immanent. But we can accept a theory of transformism in which a special intervention of God takes place. In no supposition may we admit that any animal body demanded the creation of the human soul. For there is an essential difference between matter and spirit. It can indeed be said that God, Who directed evolution precisely to man as to an end, owes it to Himself to create a man by the infusion of the human soul but that this is not due to any internal exigency on the part of organic matter no matter how highly organized. It is preferable to say that an animal body evolved and was slowly formed under the direction of God to that point where it was suitable for the infusion of the spiritual soul. In this case, the soul as the form of the body, by its own information of the animal body profoundly transforms the body into which it is inserted and thus constitutes that body genuinely human. There is no great difference whether one says that the spiritual form created the last disposition within the matter by informing it under the influence of God as the efficient cause or whether one says that God Himself, logically prior, produced certain ultimate dispositions in organic matter to proximately dispose this animal body to be the material cause of a human composite. In both cases it is evident that God, by infusing the spiritual soul, disposes this organic matter so that it should become human matter. In the first opinion a body of a brute is adorned with a human soul and thus becomes human. In the second opinion, it becomes human after having been an animal but close to the human. In the second opinion, which is preferable, the whole man, body and soul, is clearly formed by the immediate operation of God. The organic matter, which is the material cause, would in this opinion have been previously animal. In the classical opinion it has been considered inorganic matter. But in both cases, matter does not become the matter of man through its innate forces but through the direct intervention of God.

Man, even with regard to his body, arises by a special intervention of God inasmuch as the infusion of a human soul induces a specifically human organization of the body, whether this humanization is conceived as rationally prior to the infusion of the soul or concomitant with it through that mutual and reciprocal causality by which the ultimate disposition for the reception of the form is affected by the presence of the form itself. It does not appear to us, from theological sources, that there is any contradiction between such theory and what the Catholic theologian is obliged to hold. Man is still essentially different from the brute, and body and soul are still formed by the immediate intervention of God.

Not every species of transformism can be admitted. Materialistic transformism, which explains the body of man by immanent intramundane forces of evolution prescinding from the activity of God, cannot be accepted by the theologian. However, if the theologian accepts the doctrine of the peculiar intervention of God in regard to the formation not only of the soul of man but also of his body, we do not see that he is in any difficulty from any magisterial text. The theories of moderate transformism could, it seems, be modestly proposed until such a moment as theology and science arrive at fuller clarity.

There is no doubt that many elements in the Genesis recital are also figurative. Among the symbolic elements may perhaps be considered the formation of man from the slime of the earth, the Garden of Paradise, the trees, the leading of the animals to man that he might give them their names, the formation of Eve from the rib of Adam, the serpent, the splendid sword, and the tunics of leaves.

As regards the formation of Eve, it is perhaps possible to interpret the text as implying formation of Eve from some part of Adam's body, or as implying that Adam is the exemplary cause of Eve, thus intimating the equality of human nature in Adam and Eve. We do not assert that this interpretation is the genuine interpretation of the formation of Eve, but we merely state negatively, that it is not evident that the narrative of Sacred Scripture forbids this interpretation. Thus Eve would be presented as the equal of Adam according to her human nature, an equality which is the basis for monogamy, but subordinate to him within the household.

The Genesis narrative obviously supposes the essential unity of the human race. The term used in describing the creation of Eve, namely, "rib" or "side," is certainly one of the most obscure words in Genesis. Man and woman form a unity, each enjoys a common nature superior to the nature of animals, each complements the other and is meant for the other. The author certainly teaches in this story of Eve the spiritual nature of womanhood and her root equality with man, and the fact that the two form a moral person according to God's design. Woman possesses the identical human nature as man and this truth is strongly underscored in the relation of her creation. It seems legitimate to suggest modestly that what is underscored here are these religious truths and that an interpretation of Adam as an exemplary cause is not forbidden. The Biblical Commission has formally stated that Eve was drawn in some way from Adam. From whatever aspect we look upon the problem, the idea that God took an animal and transformed it is somewhat artificial with respect to Eve. The furthest that we can go in suggesting a solution to this problem is that Adam was at least the exemplary cause of Eve in so far as her body and her nature were fashioned after his. The exact manner in which her body is formed is uncertain from the text, nor has tradition clarified it with any certainty.

The doctrine of the origin of all men from one pair seems to be so intimately involved with other dogmatic truths, such as the dogma of original sin, that all Catholics must hold it.[10] "No Catholic can hold that after Adam there existed on this earth true men who did

[10] V. Marcozzi, "Poligenesi ed evoluzione nelle origini dell'uomo," *Gregorianum*, 1948, p. 390. Cf. also H. Lennerz, "Quid theologo dicendum de polygenismo," *Gregorianum*, 1948, pp. 81–98.

not take their origin through natural generation from him as from the first parent of all, or that Adam is merely a symbol for a number of first parents. For it is unintelligible how such an opinion can be squared with what the sources of revealed truth and the documents of the Magisterium of the Church teach on original sin, which proceeds from sin actually committed by an individual Adam, and which, passed on to all by way of generation, is in everyone as his own." [11]

[11] This translation is taken from p. 43 of *The Encyclical "Humani Generis" with a Commentary* [by] A. C. Cotter, S.J. (2d ed.; Weston, Mass.: Weston College Press, 1952), which gives the text of this 1950 papal encyclical in the original Latin with an English translation opposite. The Latin original here runs as follows: "Cum vero de alia coniecturali opinione agitur, videlicet de polygenismo quem vocant, tum Ecclesiae filii eiusmodi libertate minime fruuntur. Non enim christifideles eam sententiam amplecti possunt quam qui retinent, asseverant vel post Adam hisce in terris veros homines exstitisse qui non ab eodem prouti omnium protoparente naturali generatione originem duxerint, vel Adam significare multitudinem quamdam protoparentum; cum nequaquam appareat quomodo huiusmodi sententia componi queat cum iis quae fontes revelatae veritatis et acta Magisterii Ecclesiae proponunt de peccato originali, quod procedit ex peccato vere commisso ab uno Adamo, quodque generatione in omnes transfusum, inest unicuique proprium." *Ibid.*, p. 42.

DARWINISM AND AMERICA

VINCENT C. HOPKINS

In 1859 when Charles Darwin published his hypothesis of evolution by natural selection as an explanation of how things had come to be in the organic world, he was unaware of the uses to which the phrases he had coined, or made current, would be put in areas beyond the properly biological. His theory, however, filled a gap in the general intellectual structure of the day. The higher criticism of the Bible had undermined the influence of the scriptural account of the origin of things and there was a rather common feeling that there was need for a new Genesis. In addition, the climate of opinion among the consciously intellectual had been becoming increasingly materialistic in the years before the publication of the *Origin of Species by Natural Selection or the Preservation of Favoured Races in the Struggle for Life.* Scientists had been allowing themselves the luxury of generalization and *vulgarisateurs*, like the German doctor Louis Büchner who proclaimed in his book, *Energy and Matter*, that "matter is immortal and for this reason it is impossible that the world can have been created," were deducing from these generalizations, with many a lyric leap, what they wished to find in them, support for mechanistic materialism. God, Who had been reduced in the thinking of the deistic *philosophes* of the eighteenth century to the role of a *fais-néant* king of the later Merovingian dynasty, was now read out of creation completely.

However, the abolition of God, as Dean Swift once remarked of a hypothetical abolition of Christianity, was not without its inconveniences in the intellectual as well as in other orders. For, in addition to mechanistic materialism, another idol of the nineteenth-century market place was the idea of progress. This idea, which is profoundly Christian in origin, had been glowingly described in secular terms in the previous century by the Marquis de Condorcet, among others, in a work which he wrote while he was in hiding during the Terror. In this book *Sketch for a Historical Picture of the Progress of the Human Mind*, Condorcet recounted the nine stages by which men had lifted themselves from savagery to the brink of perfection on earth, the tenth stage, which, so sanguine was the Marquis, apparently was soon to be reached. How men had attained this highly desirable state was explained by Condorcet in a way that was typical of his age. It had been done by Reason, the universal meliorative of that period. But this type of dualistic thinking did not sit well with the materialistic monists of the succeeding century. Something else was needed, and evolution by natural selection fitted very nicely.

Developmental hypotheses had been in circulation for some time. Buffon and Lamarck were aware of the evolution of biological species. Erasmus Darwin, Charles's grandfather, had noted the struggle for survival with a happy outcome for the fittest, and had developed an evolutionary theory to such a degree that his biographer has claimed that "for every book by the grandson there was a chapter by the grandfather." Sir Charles Lyell had published his *Principles of Geology*, the second volume of which had a great influence on Darwin, in 1830. In this work he described the uniformitarian development of the earth's strata and upset the dominant catastrophic theory. Apart from the world of science, the idea of growth had been popularized by the historians of the eighteenth century, by Montesquieu, Voltaire and Gibbon as well as Condorcet. It had been further developed by Hegel in his theory of the three stages of human history, oriental despotism, classical slavery and modern freedom, and by Comte who elaborated upon the theological, metaphysical and positivistic stages of human thinking. Indicative of

how widely such ideas had spread are the remarks Disraeli puts in
the mouth of Lady Constance, a character in his novel *Tancred*,
published in 1847: "You know, all is development—the principle is
perpetually going on. First there was nothing; then there was something; then—I forget the next—I think there were shells; then fishes;
then we came—let me see—did we come next? Never mind that;
we came at last, and the next change will be something very superior
to us, something with wings."

Evolution by natural selection, consequently, had a wide appeal
in the mid-nineteenth century. It was automatic in its operations and
so did away with any need for purpose in the universe, be it the purpose of a creator or of a creature. But apart from satisfying the
intellectual needs of that generation by bolstering an already existing deterministic materialism, the theory also mirrored the kind of
competition which was common in a world in the throes of the industrial revolution, dominated by the Protestant ethic and embarked on
imperialistic ventures. Finally, the theory of natural selection and
the arguments of the classical economists to prove that unlimited
competition brought about the best and cheapest product were very
similar.[1]

---

[1] For general descriptions of the period during which the evolutionary hy-
pothesis was in process of formation see Loren Eiseley's *Darwin's Century* (Garden
City, New York: Doubleday, 1958), Jacques Barzun's *Darwin, Marx, Wagner*
(Boston: Little, Brown & Co., 1947), and the article by Robert Scoon in
Stow Persons (ed.), *Evolutionary Thought in America* (New York: G. Braziller,
Inc., 1956). Büchner's book appeared in 1885; he followed it up with other
works in the interests of materialism. Condorcet's *Sketch* was first published in
1795. There is a recent (1955) translation of it by June Barraclough. The Count
de Buffon (1707–1788) suggested that animal species might be arranged in a
temporal series stemming from a common ancestor but he was under the impression that revealed truth taught otherwise. The Chevalier de Lamarck (1744–
1829) expressed his views in his *Zoological Philosophy*. His evolutionary theory
is characterized by use inheritance. Erasmus Darwin's (1731–1802) highly original ideas are contained in his *Zoonomia* and in a poem, "The Loves of the
Plants" of which there is a parody in the *Anti-Jacobin* entitled "The Loves of
the Triangles." The statement about Erasmus Darwin is from E. Krause, *Erasmus
Darwin*, trans. W. S. Dallas (London, 1879), p. 132. Barzun describes the use
of the idea of growth by eighteenth-century historians and publicists in the work
referred to above, pp. 38 ff. Hegel's theory is contained in his *The Philosophy of
History*; Comte's in his *Discours sur l'Esprit Positif* (1844). Scoon cites the
passage from Disraeli's *Tancred* in the article mentioned above, p. 13.

It is with the social aspects of the influence of Darwin's ideas, particularly in the United States, that we shall attempt to deal here. Darwin did not apply his theory to human society in a systematic form. This was done by Herbert Spencer who had already written along evolutionary lines in his book *Progress: Its Law and Cause* which had been published in 1857. In that period individualism, complete liberty, was the current liberalism, and the more advanced shared Spencer's views on the role of the state as they had been set forth in his book, *The Man Versus the State*, of 1884. The state was to be restricted for all practical purposes to keeping the peace, and individuals were to be left as free as possible as they competed for the various rewards that were available. This idea of the purpose of civil society fitted quite well with the Darwinian picture of life among the plants and animals, and the latter had considerable influence on Spencer's thought as that was elaborated in his *Synthetic Philosophy*. According to Spencer, life progressed from incoherent homogeneity, the protozoa, to a coherent heterogeneity, the higher animals and man. The final result of this process was civil society in which, as in the organisms, a state of equilibrium was eventually to be achieved which Spencer described as being one of "the greatest perfection and the most complete happiness."

This system of thought in which, apparently, deterministic materialism and the idea of progress were reconciled, was much better received in the United States than it was in England. Spencer's individualism and optimism were very congenial to American minds nurtured on the theology of the dissenting denominations, many of them millennial in character, which had stressed the desirability of no organization, or as little as possible, in matters spiritual. In particular, the ideas contained in Spencer's writings were highly satisfactory to the men who were exploiting, or who hoped to be able to exploit, the resources of the country in the years after the Civil War. They had no desire to be hampered by government, though they were not averse to having government assist them. It might be said that Spencer told many an American of that day what he wanted to hear and he told it to him in the language of science at a time when that

idiom carried great prestige and when the intellectual roots of traditional Protestantism were withering.

The American business scene in the seventies and eighties of the
nineteenth century, with its Vanderbilts, Goulds, Drews, Fisks, bore
a close resemblance to the world Darwin had described. It was an
era of intense competition in which the prizes went to the strong and,
in many cases, the unscrupulous. It is not surprising that, while the
average businessman was not given to rationalization, the ideas put
in circulation by Darwin and Spencer should have been made use of
by the more reflective among them. Rockefeller echoed them in a
speech when he explained to his hearers that the growth of a large
business was merely "the survival of the fittest." Using the analogy
of the American Beauty rose which could "be produced in the splen-
dor and fragrance which bring cheer to its beholder only by sacrific-
ing the early buds" which grew around it, he pointed out that the
building up of a great corporation by a similar process was but "the
working out of a law of nature and a law of God." Andrew Carnegie,
who did for steel what Rockefeller did for oil, was a professed dis-
ciple of Spencer and he has described his earnest wish to meet him,
one that was gratified, for, he wrote, "seldom has one been more
deeply indebted than I to him and Darwin." Not only did evolution
free him from "theology and the supernatural," it also provided the
premises for his book of essays, *The Gospel of Wealth*. Writing of
the "Law of Competition," he admitted that it was "sometimes hard
on the individual" but maintained that it was "best for the race"
because it ensured "the survival of the fittest in every department."
So he welcomed "as conditions to which we must accommodate ourselves" great inequality of environment, the concentration of business, industrial and commercial, in the hands of a few and "the law
of competition between these as being not only beneficial, but essential to the future progress of the race." Chauncey Depew, the railroad lawyer, senator from New York and well-known after-dinner
speaker, gave voice to the same sentiments when he stated that the
guests at the great dinners in New York represented the survival of

the fittest and James J. Hill, who should have known, declared that the law of the railroad business was the survival of the fittest.[2]

It is not surprising that the ideas entertained by the leading businessmen of the century should have had their effect on the thinking of their lawyers and, through them, on the law of the land. This was largely done by giving the phrase "due process of law" a Spencerian meaning. The phrase, which has a history reaching back to Magna Carta at least, had been incorporated into the first section of the Fourteenth Amendment to the Constitution which had been ratified in 1868. This amendment had been prompted by doubts concerning the constitutionality of the Civil Rights Act of 1866 which had barely been passed over President Johnson's veto. By means of the first section of the amendment citizens of the United States were to be protected against infringements of their liberties by state governments. The interpretation of this section of the amendment began in 1873 when the Slaughter House Cases were heard by the Supreme Court. The lawyer for the plaintiffs, ex-Justice of the Supreme Court John A. Campbell, argued that the monopoly of slaughtering given the Crescent City Company of New Orleans by the legislature of Louisiana violated the first section of the Fourteenth Amendment and so was unconstitutional. After having cited Adolphe Thiers' book *Property*, Turgot, Tocqueville, the historian Buckle, the political scientist Lieber, Lord Macaulay and Coke's report on the Case of Monopolies of 1601, all against such concessions and in favor of liberty of trade, Campbell contended that the purpose of the first section of the amendment was not only to protect the freed Negroes in their newly acquired rights but also to give constitutional embodiment to the theory of *laissez-faire* individualism. It had been free-

[2] Rockefeller's Sunday School Address is cited by Richard Hofstadter in his *Social Darwinism in American Thought* (rev. ed.; Boston: Beacon Press, 1955), p. 31, from William Ghent's *Our Benevolent Feudalism* (New York: The Macmillan Co., 1902). Carnegie's remarks are contained in his *Autobiography* (Boston: Houghton Mifflin Co., 1920), p. 327, and in his *Gospel of Wealth* (London: F. C. Hagen and Co., 1889), pp. 3–6. Depew's statement is taken from his *My Memories of Eighty Years* (New York: C. Scribner's Sons, 1922), pp. 383–84. Hill's remark is cited by Hofstadter, *op. cit.*, p. 31.

dom, he asserted, "free action, free enterprise—free competition" that the colonizers of the future United States had sought when they had come to the eastern shores of North America. The monopoly granted to the Crescent City Company abridged the privileges and immunities of the citizens of the United States, it deprived them of liberty and the equal protection of the laws. These rights had been guaranteed to all citizens of the United States by the Fourteenth Amendment and it was the duty of the court to declare invalid the act of the legislature of Louisiana which had created a monopoly and violated those rights.

The majority of the Supreme Court declined to accept this novel line of reasoning and left the slaughterers of New Orleans who were not connected with the Crescent City Company without relief for a number of years. The voice of the future, however, was heard in the dissents of Justice Stephen Field and Justice Joseph Bradley who adopted Campbell's position and developed it further. It would take a number of years before the Supreme Court would make such an interpretation of the due process clause of the Fourteenth Amendment its own and when it did it would be due in no small part to the efforts of Field who was really more an exponent of the individualism indigenous to the United States than a convert to Spencerian or Darwinian formulas.

An important step toward the court's adoption of such an interpretation was taken in 1885 when the witty and distinguished William Maxwell Evarts appeared before the New York Court of Appeals in a case which involved the validity of a statute of the New York legislature which, as a health measure, forbade the manufacture of cigars in tenement houses. Evarts argued that the law violated the first section of the Fourteenth Amendment because it deprived, unduly, the cigar makers of their liberty to work where they wanted. In his brief he cited the opinions of Field and Bradley in the Slaughter House Cases and the argument of Campbell. Judge Earl, speaking for the court, supported Evarts' contentions and backed up the court's judgment with the opinions of Field and Bradley and by references to Adam Smith's *Wealth of Nations,* the Darwinian theory of the struggle for existence and Thomas M. Cooley's *Constitutional Limitations* which by 1885 was in its sixth edition. The drift of this work was that the police power of the state was to be confined as straitly as possible in the interests of individual liberty, especially in the economic sphere. "Freedom," the court said, citing Cooley, "is the general rule and restraint the exception." The opinion of the New York Court of Appeals in this case, known as *in re* Jacobs, was soon adopted by the courts of Pennsylvania, Massachusetts, Illinois, Colorado, Missouri, Kansas, Ohio and West Virginia.

The organization of the American Bar Association in 1878 was also effective in spreading Spencerian ideas throughout the bench and bar of the country. Its roster was a very distinguished one. Campbell, Cooley, Evarts and his partner Joseph H. Choate, David Brewer, the nephew of Justice Field and soon to be his companion in arms on the Supreme Court, Christopher Tiedeman whose *Limitations of the Police Power* supplemented Cooley's work, William H. Taft and many others. The papers and addresses of this organization drove home the doctrines of *laissez-faire* individualism, with or without the Spencerian formulas, again, again and again.

The adoption of a Darwinian interpretation of the clauses of the Fourteenth Amendment by the state courts and the leading lawyers of the day was bound to have its effect on the members of the Supreme Court of the United States. Also, the personnel of the Court changed a great deal between 1888 and 1898. When the Court in 1905, through Justice Peckham, invalidated a New York statute which limited the hours of work in bakeries to ten hours a day because such an exercise of the police power infringed on the liberties of workers in bakeries, Spencerian ideas had won the day.

It was in his dissent to this opinion that Justice Holmes remarked, "The Fourteenth Amendment does not enact Mr. Herbert Spencer's *Social Statics.*" Despite the justice's dictum, it would appear that a majority of the court thought it did just that and would continue in that opinion for many years to come. The result was that what is called social legislation was continually invalidated by the courts in the name of a theory which conceived unlimited competition, and not the common good, to be the end of civil society.[3]

Darwinism also had its effects on international relations. In that area, combined with the idea of race it provided a rationalization for the imperialistic ventures of the Western nations in the late nineteenth and early twentieth centuries. This idea of race, to a great extent the fusion of the linguistic findings of the philologists with the physical classifications of the anthropologists, had been popularized by, among others, Count Joseph Arthur de Gobineau whose *Essay on the Inequality of Races* appeared in 1853, six years before the publication of the *Origin of Species*. But Darwinism and a theory of race were hardly contradictory and such ideas as the survival of the fittest could be tailored to racist patterns on the human level without much difficulty. As Aubrey Menen has remarked in his *Dead Man in the Silver Market*, "Men of all races have always sought for a convincing explanation of their own excellence, and they have frequently found what they were looking for." So the late nineteenth century and the early twentieth saw the appearance of various theories to the effect that by natural selection it was predestined that certain races should ascend the evolutionary tree and that others, owing to their lack of the qualities which led to survival, should fall behind and ultimately be taken over by their betters for their own good. This theory could be given a theistic turn as was done by the Midwestern Congregationalist minister Josiah Strong in his book *Our Country*, published in 1885. In this work, a blend of the idea of race, of Darwinian ideas, of the myth of Anglo-Saxon superiority and of the Puritan idea of mission, Strong urged his fellow countrymen to allow the mighty centrifugal tendencies inherent in the Anglo-

---

[3] Campbell's argument is analyzed by Benjamin Twiss in his *Lawyers and the Constitution* (Princeton: Princeton University Press, 1942), pp. 42–62, and by E. S. Corwin in his *Liberty against Government* (Baton Rouge: Louisiana State University Press, 1948), p. 119. For the opinions of the judges in the Slaughter House Cases see 16 *Wallace* 36 ff. *In re* Jacobs can be found in 98 *New York Reports* 98. The bakery case is Lochner v. New York, 198 *United States Reports* 45 ff.

Saxon stock full play over the rest of the world. Before their trium-
phant advance unfit, inferior races were bound to give way as the
American Indian had. Such ideas were popularized by politicians
like Senator Albert Beveridge of Indiana. In a typical statement he
once said that the late President Grant "never forgot that we are a
conquering race and that we must obey our blood and occupy new
markets and, if necessary, new lands. He (Grant) had the prophet's
seer-like sight which beheld, as part of the Almighty's infinite plan,
the disappearance of debased civilization and decaying races before
the higher civilization of the nobler and more virile types of men."
The conclusion to this and much more fustian was that the United
States should hold and govern the Philippine Islands. Such ideas
also influenced the thought of the naval historian Alfred Thayer
Mahan, whose works, beginning in 1890 with *The Influence of Sea
Power upon History, 1660–1873*, so impressed the military of the
various countries of the world during this period. These ideas also
loomed large in the propaganda of the Immigration Restriction
League which was organized in 1894 and they were the main arguments advanced in favòr of the restriction of immigration in the
1920's. Madison Grant, a New York lawyer, was most active in
spreading racist ideas. He published a book, *The Passing of the
Great Race*, in 1916. According to Grant, races varied greatly in
quality and only superior races, like the Nordic, were capable of
founding great civilizations. Racial purity, he stated, echoing Gobineau, was essential to human endeavor and ethnic intermixture led
to decay. Applying this idea to the United States, Grant depicted the
descendants of the seventeenth- and eighteenth-century immigrants
as the country's saving remnant. Their ancestors had been Nordics and
it was they who founded the present greatness of the country. Immigration, by allowing inferior races into the country, had already
sapped the pristine vigor of the American population. It was about
to overwhelm the ever-narrowing Nordic element and should be
stopped. The fittest apparently need more than natural selection to
survive.

As Loren Eiseley has remarked, Darwin, while not responsible for the grosser philosophical sins of some of his followers, did incorporate into the *Origin of Species* a powerful expression of the utilitarian philosophy of his time. He devoted very little attention to the forces in nature leading to cooperation and emphasized selfish motivation. The strain of pessimistic determinism which was current in his time was fully reflected in his writings. He leaned heavily on the gloomy prognostications of Thomas Malthus as they were set forth in the *Essay on the Principle of Population as It Affects the Future Improvement of Society with Remarks on the Speculations of Mr. Godwin, M. Condorcet and Others,* which first appeared in 1798. The previous century had been unduly optimistic and the pendulum was swinging far to the other extreme. A passionate Darwinian like Edward L. Youmans could solemnly assure the reformer Henry George that there was absolutely nothing he could do about graft in New York City but wait—he did not say whether in this world or the next—for natural selection to take its course. Evolution also, as Eiseley comments, "is an idea that has seemed to many to condemn man to the life of a beast and there are those who have ordered their days accordingly." But this has not been the only fruit of the evolutionary hypothesis, generally understood, and not as Spencer reworked it and applied it to society. There is a dynamic as well as a static aspect of the idea and the open universe of James and Bergson, the Heraclitean interpretation as opposed to the Parmenidean, became a basis for the arguments of those who thought that something could be done besides waiting for the operations of natural selection.[4]

[4] Menen's observation is on p. 1 of the work mentioned. The citation from Beveridge can be found in Claude Bowers, *Beveridge and the Progressive Era* (Boston: Houghton Mifflin Co., 1932), p. 68. Eiseley's remarks are contained in the work mentioned, pp. 348 ff. The encounter between George and Youmans is described by the former in his *A Perplexed Philosopher* which is cited by Hofstadter, *op. cit.,* p. 34.

EVOLUTION AND CYCLICISM IN OUR TIME

WALTER J. ONG

There can be no doubt that the discovery of the process of evolution, cosmic and organic, has been one of the greatest achievements of the human mind. In a sense, this is the central discovery in the Western world since Renaissance times, and in a still further sense it is the central corporate discovery of all mankind.

The discovery of cosmic and organic evolution is part of man's discovery of himself in history. Early man had no effective way of putting together really extended history. Preliterate man could not control enough data to enable him to reconstruct a lengthy sequence of events in time. There had been, of course, data gathered and reported by eyewitnesses, but when this information had been passed on through even a few generations without the help of writing, fact —provided one had it in the first place—became inextricable from fictional accretion. Instead of a historical account of their past, preliterate peoples even today have only myth, related perhaps to fact at certain points but related so erratically as to make full historical reconstruction impossible.

With the invention and spread of writing, extended records began to create a new and important dimension in human thinking. As records accumulated, it was only a matter of time until persons would begin to notice that the state of affairs in the past had been quite different from what it was in the present. In their hieroglyphic writing the ancient Egyptians accumulated great masses of records. The Hebrews, coeval with the later Egyptians, and, if in some ways less civilized, still advanced beyond the Egyptians in possessing the alphabet, had a far-developed historical sense, as the Old Testament shows. Their way of conceiving history is not so developed as ours, yet they have an unmistakable historical instinct and outlook. In Aristotle's day, when alphabetic writing was probably only about fifteen hundred years old, the historical dimension has begun to intrude even in scientific thinking. Near the beginning of his *Metaphysics* Aristotle inserts a quite sketchy and primitive, and yet portentous history of philosophy.

From the ancient Mediterranean civilizations, modern man's sense of history develops in a rather direct line through medieval and Renaissance European civilization into the age of the Enlightenment and thence into the present one world, where it is now in one way or another shared by all men. In this line of development, the sense of a past accessible through circumstantial records grew in the human consciousness as it had never grown at other earlier times or in other civilizations. In the Chinese civilization, perhaps because of the different kind of commitment to time involved in character writing as against alphabetic writing, perhaps because of specialization in other awarenesses made possible by this same remarkable character writing, perhaps because of relative lack of contact with the Hebrew and Christian religious sense of time, or because of all these factors and some others as well, so strong a historical sense did not develop. The Chinese would have to acquire this sense later from the West, most forcefully in its Marxist manifestation.

Other civilizations, too, performed more like the Chinese than like the Western segment of mankind. The Hindu, the Central American, the African did not themselves develop the modern sense of a temporal dimension in the cosmos. These and other civilizations have learned this, with modern science, from the West. The margin by which the West outdistanced other civilizations in achieving this sense of history, however, has been in reality slight. If man has been here for some four hundred thousand years, the segment of mankind which first developed this historical sense did not begin to do so until nearly all this four hundred thousand years had elapsed—that is, until roughly some three thousand years ago.

What we mean by this historical sense should be noted carefully. By the eighteenth century in the West, when this sense had pretty well matured, what had happened was not simply that man had become speculatively interested in time. Speculative interest in time he had had for centuries. Nor was it that man had developed a sense of reality as embedded in a flow of time such as Heraclitus had registered six centuries before Christ in his logion, *Panta rhei,* or "All things are in flux." A sense of flux is an old awareness, too. What had happened by the age of the Enlightenment was that man had achieved a sense that the present he knew was growing out of a past with which he was in some kind of verifiable contact and which was different from the present, and that this same present was pointed into a future destined itself to be vastly different from both the present and the past. Today we are taught from elementary school on, that earlier ages of the universe differed vastly from later ones, and this notion has become so commonplace that we find it hard to imagine human beings unaware of it. Yet it is safe to say that until quite recent generations most human beings were generally unaware of this fact. Man could become aware of it only when he had methods of probing into the past far enough and accurately enough to be struck by the changes between one period and another, in human culture, learning, and finally in physical and cosmic environment.

By the time of Diderot's *Pensées sur l'interprétation de la nature* in 1754, the sense of a present involved in a past and future vastly different from itself and from one another is manifestly part of the informed Western outlook:

Could not the philosopher . . . suspect that life had its individual elements scattered and mixed in the mass of matter; that it happened that these elements united because it was possible for this to happen; that the embryo formed of these elements has passed through an in-

finitude of organization and development; that it has acquired in succession movement, sensation, ideas, thought, reflection, conscience [*conscience* in the original French, which means either consciousness or
conscience but seems to signify the latter here], feelings, emotions, signs,
gestures, sounds, articulation, language, laws, sciences, and arts; that
millions of years have elapsed between each of these developments; that
there are perhaps other developments to be undergone and other paths
of growth to be followed which are as yet unknown to us.[1]

This passage from Diderot and other passages quoted in H. F.
Osborn, *From the Greeks to Darwin,* can serve to remind us that
perhaps the ultimate triumph to date of the evolutionary outlook is
the knowledge that the evolutionary outlook itself was arrived at by
an evolutionary process. Diderot is writing over a century before
Charles Darwin's great work, *Origin of Species,* and yet it is no dis-
credit to Darwin's genius to state that, given the awareness evident in
the Diderot passage, the discovery of the principle of natural selection,
not only in its primordial Darwinian form but also in its later modifications and refinements was only a matter of time. The insight
which Darwin was to crystallize in his work, so brilliantly and scru-
pulously written and so often painstakingly revised, and to make current with the aid of his remarkable gift for catch phrases—"origin
of species," "natural selection," "survival of the fittest," [2] "struggle
for life," to name only a few—was not entirely his own. This insight
was itself evolving in the minds of men as they passed on from generation to generation their accumulated records of past experience
and their growing reflections on what they knew of the past.

Indeed, by some strange sort of fatality, the very origin of the
Origin of Species provides evidence of the most explicit and spectacular sort concerning the corporate and gradual origin of human discoveries. For a great many of Darwin's most original insights were
on his own humble admission arrived at by at least one other individ-

[1] Diderot, *Pensées sur l'interprétation de la nature,* LVII, 2, in *Oeuvres
complètes de Diderot,* ed. J. Assézat and Maurice Tourneux (Paris, 1875–77),
II, 57–58. The translation of this passage in H. F. Osborn, *From the Greeks to
Darwin* (New York and London: Charles Scribner's Sons, 1929), pp. 171–72,
varies at points from the French text which I have translated here, but not significantly in connection with the present issue.

[2] Attributed to Spencer as its originator, but used by Darwin in later editions
of the *Origin of Species.*

ual at the same time in the same intellectual milieu. The correspondence in 1858 between Darwin and the somewhat younger Alfred Russel Wallace is a commonplace item in the history of ideas. In it we can see the convergence of the two men's individual lights in the theory of natural selection, made explicit in their famous joint communication to the Linnean Society. The case alerts us to a state of affairs which other cases confirm: discoveries are not so much stumbled upon as developed. Knowledge itself is a communal affair and evolves communally. The most an individual can hope to contribute to the process is what we have recently learned to style a "break-through" in a front of activity which must be on the whole cooperative rather than purely personal. Because it develops communally, the structure of human knowledge must be explained not only in terms of its various logics. It must also be explained sociologically. The accounts of Henry Ford or Thomas Alva Edison or Max Planck or Albert Einstein working out utterly new inventions all by themselves—normally in cold and ill-lighted attics—belong with Horatio Alger literature or the old Tom Swift books. Reality is something different.

II

When we look behind the Darwin-Wallace correspondence to the discoveries and reflections of men who preceded them, we find even more unmistakably how thoroughly their great discovery or "break-through" was dependent on the painstaking work, brilliant intellectual risks, and brilliant insights of others and how much it was dependent also upon obscure and individually uncontrollable, but immensely influential, psychological and sociological forces of which Darwin's own age could hardly be explicitly aware since we are only now learning to identify them.[3]

Evolutionary thinking can be discerned taking dim but real shape

[3] See Robert Scoon, "The Rise and Impact of Evolutionary Ideas," in *Evolutionary Thought in America*, edited by Stow Persons (New York: George Braziller, Inc., 1956), pp. 4–42. Many of the instances which I give of the general diffusion of ideas contributing to or connected with evolutionary thinking before Darwin or in the milieu surrounding Darwin can be found discussed in this collection of studies or in the many specialized monographs referred to in the notes to the various studies.

in the philosophy and science of the rather remote pre-Darwinian age and in a general build-up of the historical dimension of all thinking. In his *Scienza nuova* Giambattista Vico (1668–1744) focuses attention on development, and this focus is intensified in philosophical thought through Hegel (1770–1831) and Schelling (1775–1854). Auguste Comte (1798–1857) proposed a philosophy built on considerable knowledge of social development as well as on massive theories about the nature of this development. Karl Marx's 1848 *Communist Manifesto* involves still more theories about the nature and inevitability of change, social and other.

Evolutionary thinking was found taking shape at an early date not only in philosophy itself but also in the natural sciences, which even as late as the nineteenth century were regarded, as they were through the Middle Ages and the Renaissance, as part of philosophy, as "natural philosophy." The German philosopher Kant (1724–1804), like the French astronomer Laplace (1749–1827), faced into the problems of the cosmos as it was known to the new astronomy and proposed nebular hypotheses to account for the present state of the universe by a theory of stellar evolution. Descartes and Leibnitz had already bruited abroad the idea that the earth could have gone through a molten stage. When proposed as conjectures by early cosmologists, such unfamiliar stages had tended to be explained as aberrations or catastrophes. But in the eighteenth and the nineteenth centuries the English geologists James Hutton (1726–97) and Charles Lyell (1797–1875) discarded the older catastrophic theories in favor of uniformitarian explanations. Catastrophism had viewed the present state of the universe as due to earlier, mysteriously violent deviations from some more pacific "natural" order. These deviations or catastrophes were supposed to be inexplicable in terms of still operating physical processes. Uniformitarianism took for granted that past states of the universe which account for present conditions are themselves explainable in terms of processes subject to the same physical laws as are now operating and verifiable.

Hutton and Lyell did not of course destroy catastrophism. Such a theory still persists in our own day in the minds of many who feel that the only cosmology possible to the devout is one which proceeds by a series of abrupt changes initiated by special interventions of God. To this mind, although the universe was evolving for billions of years toward the point where life, at least on our planet, became possible, nothing short of an abrupt divine intervention breaking sharply with earlier processes can account for the appearance of the first living organisms. In this catastrophic view, although the first human remains in the five- or ten-billion-year history of our universe appear after the patient elaboration over billions of years first of larger and larger molecules out of which organic substances can be synthesized and then of more and more highly developed organisms which finally approximate man in external form, and although these first human remains appear in the very epoch when the organisms approximating man were in full developmental career, one must conceive of the human body as having nothing to do with this stupendous cosmic process. Rather, one must imagine it as being formed quite suddenly from those materials alone—various aluminum salts or other clay-like matter—which had reached their more or less stable forms relatively early in the process of cosmic development and had not passed through any of the later organic transmutations.

The survival of catastrophism in one or another form and the tendency to link catastrophism with a religious view of the universe confused the issues in many religious circles, but it could not stop the development of evolutionary theory in the natural sciences. By the late eighteenth century Erasmus Darwin (1731–1802), Charles Darwin's grandfather, was working with the idea that species are not separated by chasms from one another but rather connected through intermediate forms in lines of descent, and Lamarck (1744–1829) had produced his theory of use inheritance which Charles Darwin's theory of natural selection superseded. At this time, the term "biology" itself, proposed independently in 1802 by Lamarck and G. R. Treviranus, came into use, so that the very science of biology, insofar as it can be considered a distinct knowledge, is itself a product of the evolutionary milieu.

In both philosophy and the natural sciences the interest in evolution was a product of the visions of history which were forming in men's minds. These visions were not very clear, and yet they were both fascinating and productive. Although they had to do with change, these new visions were not quite the same as those of the older philosophies which had been more concerned with becoming in general, with coming into being as contrasted with the act of existence. The newer visions concerned themselves with series of individual events which were each unique and yet in some sense, real but difficult to fix, a part of a pattern.

One can, of course, make a distinction between evolution and history. Evolution can refer to developments in the cosmos independent of human culture, and history can refer to developments within human culture itself. Of these two concepts, history, while in a way more constricted, is nevertheless the dominant notion in the sense that the discovery of evolution is a historical event, since it takes place in human culture and not outside. Moreover, since history is closer to him, man has approached evolution by reflection on history first, so that evolution will always remain for him something associated with history and understandable in terms of this association. Here we shall speak of history in the common intertwined sense in which it refers primarily to human history but also involves, as occasion offers, the development of the universe itself before man and since.

Determining what the pattern of history is had long disturbed men and still disturbs us. For, although there are true histories and false histories, all history is selective, so that one can have as many histories—and true ones, too—as he wishes, depending on what items one selects in one's reporting. The number of histories is potentially infinite. The difficulty in finding a pattern which is *the* pattern lodges in the fact that history, whatever else it does, never really repeats itself. Every event is unique. This is what brought Aristotle to state in his *Art of Poetry* that history is less philosophical than poetry itself, which is certainly unphilosophical enough if by philosophical one means, as Aristotle did, capable of treatment in universal terms.

The one way to cast history in these terms is to transmute its singular happenings into universals, and the readiest way to effect this transmutation is to imagine that time is cyclic and as a consequence the history of the universe is, too. That is to say, everything that is now happening has happened before an infinite number of times and will happen an infinite number of times again, so that there is really nothing singular ever possible at all. One can bolster this view by selecting details in history which, put together, form a pattern of rise and fall, waxing and waning, ascent and decline, and so on—spring, summer, autumn, winter. These cyclic patterns are of course really there, provided only that one takes note of the proper details (those which relate to such patterns) and passes by the others (those which do not).

From the time of the most ancient philosophies men have been adept at noting the proper details to discern the cyclic patterns. Cyclic views of history have apparently been the dominant views. They appear in Hindu thought, in the pre-Socratic philosophers and through the ancient Greeks generally, on down through Joachim de Flora (1145–1202) and others to Spengler and Toynbee in our own day. Cyclicism is so pervasive that it obtrudes itself unnoticed in many historians, artists, and others who often fail to advert to the fact that their frames of thought have an unmistakably cyclic cast. Thus we have cultural developments explained in terms of a New England spring, summer, Indian summer, and so on— although no winter has been acknowledged as yet. A recent literary historian, Robert E. Spiller, organizes not merely North Atlantic literature but all American literature circularly in his title *The Cycle of American Literature: An Essay in Historical Criticism* (1955), just as E. I. Watkin in his *Catholic Art and Culture* had organized the history of Western art into a classical autumn, Christian spring, medieval summer, Renaissance Indian summer, baroque autumn, and modern winter, thereby seeming to imply that either art is going to have to go completely out of existence because its possibilities are all exhausted or we are headed directly into a glorious spring.

There are many early and detailed precedents for this sort of thing. Between 1720 and 1750 Iohannes Nicolaus Funccius had published in Marburg and Lemgo his five books in Latin entitled respectively (in translation) *The Childhood, Adolescence, Imminent Old Age, Vigorous Old Age,* and *Helpless Broken-Down Old Age of the Latin Language.* This kind of construct is revealing. It works so long as one views Latin and Roman culture as not particularly derivative from anything else and as not destined to feed into anything else. The moment one regards Italian, Provençal, Catalan, French, Spanish, Portuguese, Rhaeto-Romanic and Roumanian as variants of Latin—which they are—the entire picture shifts and the rise-and-fall construct no longer accounts for the facts, since in modern French Latin is still on the rise, unless one detects a cycle in the French language as well, with similar attendant difficulties.

These cyclic patterns occur not only among historians operating in the field of belles-lettres but in the visions of painters, too. The well-known series of paintings by the English-born American Thomas Cole (1801–1848) entitled "The Course of Empire" pictures empire as existing successively in "The Savage State," "The Arcadian or Pastoral State," a state of "Consummation," a state of "Destruction" and a state of "Ruin." Cole himself writes a detailed plan aligning these paintings respectively with dawn, later morning, noonday, afternoon, and sunset. In both his paintings and his explanation, empire is an abstraction. The structure he sets forth is supposed to apply to any and all empires. That is to say, speaking more really, this structure helps determine and define what empire is. In the manifold of history one selects the details which work within this pattern, passing by those which do not, and in this way one finds oneself talking about empire.

In his brilliant book *The Myth of the Eternal Return* Mircea Eliade has exposed the psychological roots of the drive to detect among the details of history a cyclic pattern which will make plausible a totally cyclic view of time itself. Cyclic theories of time accomplish for the learned what the mythological rituals of the seasons accomplish for the intellectually unsophisticated. Both mitigate the terror of history, in which events, and most of all man's personal decisions, are set forever in an irreversible pattern.

Cyclic theories tend to cushion or distract from time's impact, dissociating time from unique acts, for in the extreme or pure cyclic view of the universe nothing is unique at all, since even our most personal decisions have been and will be made over and over again. Mythological rituals, more or less seasonal in their celebration and to this extent associated with a cyclic pattern, draw attention from real events to mythological archetypes which are not referrable to any real time. To ask an ancient Greek, for example, when, in what year of the universe, Dionysus was torn to pieces by the Maenads, would be to miss the whole point of the myth. These things took place somewhere outside time. Their extra-temporal status gave the myths their psychological value. By referring actual temporal occurrences in one way or another to them, these temporal occurrences could be disinfected of the curse of time. Pagan religious views generally register a human aversion to time, providing at least a subconscious refuge from time's evils.

By contrast the Hebrew and even more the Christian revelation presents time as a good. This point has become a commonplace one in contemporary theology, Protestant as well as Catholic. For the Hebrew, revelation, initially given to an ancestor, Abraham, who was seen quite definitely as inside history, was kept alive through a historical people, Abraham's descendants. For Christians, the Hebrew view was retained and supplemented by a more momentous historical incident, the Incarnation of the Son of God, Himself God, together with His subsequent death and resurrection—all events datable, even today, with greater surety than all but a few events of secular history. The Christian view sees Christ as anchored in time in at least three ways. First, like other men, He is born and dies at one certain time and no other. But secondly, unlike other men, He appears at the maturing of a special long-term development which calls for His appearance. He is expected as other men are not. He culminates the history of the Chosen People by putting an end to an intent wait of centuries. And thirdly, the centuries-long history of this Chosen People was itself, according to the common Christian teaching, not only a wait or watchful preparation but also a prefiguration or foreshadowing of His own life and work.

Thus faced squarely into time and at home in it, the Christian as such has no need for either mythological archetypes or cyclic theories of the sort studied by Eliade. Yet we do find both these pagan phenomena widespread among certain Christian populations. Notably, in medieval European culture biography is written according to these patterns. The medieval saint's life is too frequently fitted to a pre-existent archetypal pattern in which even the points at which the miracles are supposed to occur are predetermined, and the familiar secular biography such as is found in the *Mirror for Magistrates* or Lydgate's *Fall of Princes* is often based on a spectacularly cyclic design, the wheel of Fortune. When such pagan patterns occur among Christians, they can be regarded as pagan survivals. With the Renaissance the foundations were laid for a more Christian approach to biography, which would center attention on the shaping action of the human will and its decisions under grace.

Modern theology has come to speak of the Christian (and Hebrew) sense of time as "linear" rather than cyclic. Oscar Cullmann and many others have made much of this view. The concept of linearity has its disadvantages here, for the Christian and Hebrew sense of time is by no means so spatialized as the term "linear" suggests. It is more interior and psychological, or "human," and, besides, it does involve certain considerations which, when they are handled geometrically, are best handled by analogy not with straight lines but with circles, as Père Gaston Fessard has shown in his brilliant study *La dialectique des Exercices spirituels de Saint Ignace de Loyola*. Nevertheless, there is a sense in which the Christian and Hebrew sense of time can be said to be linear by contrast with cyclic views. For the Christian the soul's journey through time is a development: the soul starts out in one state and ends in quite a different one in which its career or spiritual evolution has fixed it. In a parallel fashion, the Hebrew and Christian world vision sees the universe in linear time: contrary to the conviction of Aristotle and a host of others, matter is not eternal, but the universe is created in one state and at the end of time will somehow be transfigured, different from what it has been. Christ is incarnate at a certain point in time, and this point is never reached again.

It is true that earlier Christians were ignorant of the full dimensions of cosmic time. As late as St. Robert Bellarmine and even later, we find theologians and others as well quite convinced that from the creation of the world to the expected end of time was a matter of some six thousand years, and the first Christians had done their thinking, it seems, in an even more telescoped temporal world view. It is likewise true that earlier Christians had no idea of the fact that the universe was actually evolving from day to day during their own lives, if on a scale so disproportionate to a single human life that no one person alone could be directly aware of the changes going on. What is important, however, in the Christian tradition is not the statistical errors or observational deficiencies of earlier Christians, but the total frame of mind which Christian teaching fosters. The Church herself has never been specific about the age or life expectancy of the present universe or about its day-to-day stability. Chiliasm in various forms has been recurrent, it is true, but always as an aberration. Hence, despite the defects of the world view in which Christians conceived revelation to be operating, the way for an evolutionary view was as a matter of fact kept open by Christian teaching. For in any view, however otherwise scientifically erroneous, a Christian who followed the teachings of the Catholic Church had to allow for a beginning of the universe and an ending which was different from the beginning. This sense of difference between beginning and end is congenial to evolutionary views. Cyclic views of time and the universe are not, even though they may project time patterns over millions or billions of years, as some pagan cosmologies have done.

III

When one reviews in the larger perspective suggested here the developments in thought and in world outlook which precede and accompany the work of Charles Darwin, one is struck by certain relationships between the evolutionary outlook and Christianity. The two seem curiously congenial to each other. The evolutionary outlook has grown up in an intellectual setting prepared by Christianity under the influence of the time sense which Christianity very really if not always with full consciousness encourages. For, like the Christian view, the evolutionary view involves a certain "linear" rather than cyclic sense of time.

The discovery of evolution has opened a vision of the universe which at the beginning is in a condition from which it departs never to return. The progressive changes in the cosmos, moreover, do not consist simply in a running down, as was thought when the second law of thermodynamics, the Carnot-Clausius law, was taken as the ultimate determinant of cosmic activity. According to this law, the universe is tending toward a state of complete equilibrium. The mountains will all eventually wash into the sea, hot things will lose heat to cooler things until all are of a uniform temperature, and so on. We know now that the story is more complicated than this. There is also a winding-up process in the universe, the process according to which life evolves upward in more and more complex, more and more intense forms. For, although there is some regressive organic evolution, the pattern of life on the whole is certainly one of progress.

Life is a struggle upward, a struggle against odds, but on the whole a victorious process. This conviction lies back of Darwinian and other evolutionary views in which the whole of organic evolution is a kind of ascesis, a struggle from worse to better, curiously like the career of the Christian soul. Indeed, it is not difficult to show that Christian asceticism, subtly transmuted, has formed much of the framework for Darwin's thinking. This is all the more interesting when one recalls that this same framework could not be provided by many other religions which regard life as a process in which one relaxes his hold on himself to lose himself finally in some dissolution.

But does what we know of cosmic evolution really accord with Christianity by rigidly excluding the possibility of cyclic time? Is not a throbbing universe possible, and does not such a universe involve cyclic time? That is to say, speaking in a somewhat oversimplified fashion, could it not be that the present expanding universe arose from the explosion of some sort of super-atom and that this universe will ultimately contract into the super-atom only to explode again, and so on indefinitely, so as to give us an infinite series of successive universes? And does not all this suggest cyclic time, with the same events recurring infinitely?

It would seem not. The discovery of evolution has undermined cyclic views even more than would at first blush appear. In the universe as we now know it, there exists no real model or analogue for cyclicism—that is, for identical and inevitable repetition of an event at two (much less at an infinite number of) points in time.

The grossest model for cyclicism is and has been the path of the earth around the sun. The old cyclic myths and cyclic cosmologies had assumed the permanence of the earth-sun relationship, which they commonly conceived in terms of a path of the sun around the earth. But today we know this relationship is not permanent. The path of the earth around the sun is by no means stable. It has come into being by a series of changes, and continues to undergo evolution at a rate which is measurable, although quite disproportionate to the span of human life. No season is, as a matter of fact, quite like any other, and in their succession, although there are so-called cycles of approximate repetitions, the over-all pattern is that of a one-directional change.

Even if the universe is expanding as the result of a primordial explosion of some sort of super-atom (as George Gamow and others conjecture), and if one assumes that it will eventually contract back into the super-atom only to explode and begin evolving again, all the indications we have from the world-in-time-around-us would suggest that, if we face into real particulars and details, the second of these two evolutions would be not the same as the first, but different from it somewhat as year differs from year, or one chain of evolution (European fauna and flora) differs from another (American fauna and flora). One assumes that two successive cosmic evolutions would be identical on the suspicion that they are like two successive years or eras; but we know now that two successive years or eras are not quite identical. One can set up a mathematical model for cyclic succession, of course, but there remains the problem of finding something in reality which at least hints that reality accords with the mathematical model. Nothing appears to be available. It appears that cyclic theories of cosmic evolution and of history depend upon setting up such a model or construct, for which one can find no exact counterpart anywhere in the universe, and upon using this model, despite everything, as though it applied to reality.

Perhaps it should be added that the highly poetic continuous creation theory put forth by Professor Fred Hoyle seems to leave even less room for exact repetition of events than any of the theories it proposes to replace. It is designed to counteract the Carnot-Clausius law rather than to contradict the view that individual things are different in the end from in the beginning. In this theory, although the universe as a whole does not begin all at once, every assignable item in it most certainly does begin and move through irreversible developmental states. The "background material" continuously created for the formation of clouds of interstellar gas and galaxies is certainly different at the time of its creation from what it is afterwards.

Cyclicism is even further disqualified when one considers something further about the evolution of the cosmos which is all too often left out of consideration. That is that the cosmos gives birth to the human person in its utter particularity and uniqueness. Cosmologies which view the physical universe without regard to the fact that it has given birth to the human person are not only incomplete but impossibly distorted and misleading. Too often a cosmology accounts to some degree of satisfaction for everything except human beings, who appear as some sort of monstrous intrusion on the scene. This is true even when a cosmology does account in some way for the evolution of the human body, explaining its relationship to, and probable line of development from, prehuman forms. For, frequently enough, such a cosmology lets the matter go at that, failing even to ask the question as to what the human person, this mysterious self, this interiority, inviolable, known only to me and to God, has to do with the process of cosmic evolution. For it certainly has something to do with this evolution. The universe prepared itself for some five or ten billion years for the advent of just this mysterious self, this interiority, this uniqueness which I am—and which every human being is. How is the process of cosmic evolution related to me?

Both the Christian and the pagan must face this question. And up to the present seldom has either done so. Indeed, it seems that neither knows how to do so as yet. Yet the fact is that the development of the universe to date has had direction and that the direction leads not up to or around or parallel to but into the human consciousness itself. Cosmic evolution has certainly been a process of greater and greater complexification or interiorization of existent things. Whatever of the various theories regarding the initial stages of our universe we may favor, we know that there was a time when the matter of which our globe is composed was simply too hot to make it possible for anything more complicated than simple inorganic molecules to exist—probably for a time too hot for even molecules to exist at all, so that everything was retained in a simple atomic structure. Cooling made possible the formation of crystals, organized according to a pattern which is interior in that it is determined by the internal molecular structure of the crystal but which is not very intensely interior in the sense that a crystalline structure is open: it tends to hook on to its borders further molecules without any particular limit. As the earth cools still more and the present continents and seas take shape, the gigantic protein molecules form. Despite their relatively massive sizes, these molecules are more organized in terms of an interior than are the molecules making up inorganic crystals. They do not grow by simple accretion, but have their own peculiar structural equilibrium to maintain without accretion. Their interior exists in a state of tension with the exterior around them. It seems that some of the protein molecules, or some of the things very close to them such as viruses, are able to reproduce themselves, not out of their own substance but by generating next to themselves, in certain media with which they may be surrounded, others like themselves. Higher forms of organization, which are generally regarded as properly living, have a still higher interiorizing component. Out of their interior organization, they generate other beings with their own interior organizations. The build-up of interiority reaches its maximum in man, who has the reproducing capacity of lower forms of life plus an interior and transcendent awareness of self which is so peculiarly his own that it cannot be communicated to others. But inside this awareness communication with others can take place. Indeed communication in human society, although it uses external media of all sorts, is basically a transaction between two or more unique and inviolable interiors.

This is a most inadequate sketch of incredibly complex and beautiful stages in cosmic development. But it may help to convey a sense of the way in which the human person is not adventitious but in a very profound sense native to the material universe. Each human soul, it is true, is created by a direct act of God. When I reflect on the interior self which I am, examine this sense of "I" which I alone have, it yields no evidence that it is descended from anything at all. I alone know what it feels like to be myself. Even my father and mother have not known what it feels like to be me. They have no direct consciousness of me such as my own consciousness of myself, nor do I have any direct consciousness of them. To say that my soul, as evidenced to me in my conciousness, is "descended" or derived from these or any other souls has no meaning. This "I" is unique and inaccessible. This isolation of each person, his being on his own, underived from other consciousnesses, is the glory and the terror of human existence. I cannot be duplicated even in the intelligence of another man, as I should have to be were he to know me as immediately as I know myself. Moreover, I know my uniqueness and induplicability in simply knowing myself as I do. With some three billion people in the world, no person in complete possession of his faculties is in the least worried that one of the other three billion will turn out to be a duplication of himself. The present population figure could be doubled or squared without occasioning the slightest alarm on this score. No man is an island, and yet each possesses himself alone. Each of these individual selves is the product of a direct act of God which is truly "special" in the sense that it brings into existence a special soul and consciousness, which will always remain unlike every other, a true person.

And yet these persons are born of the universe in which they live. They do not arise outside it. Matter is prepared for the human soul not merely by the body of a mother and a father; long before any human generation becomes even thinkable, it has to be organized by the evolution of the entire universe over a period of billions of years. For the material things around us, the inorganic matter and even more the organic matter from which we derive our nourishment, are not constitutive of the material universe in its primitive state. Primitive atomic matter must be elaborated by mighty cosmic forces which simultaneously distribute it into the galaxies and solar systems of today and give it the progressively higher and higher interior organization which produces the complex chemical forms with which we are surrounded and inside which we must live. The material in our bodies is billions of years old, and during these billions of years it has not been lying about in a relatively stable condition as had been supposed by Western man up until some few hundred years ago, when the material things around us had been regularly explained in terms of varying combinations of the stable elements earth, water, air, and fire. Built up of these, things were differentiated, it had been thought, without reference to time, by specific natures. Today we know that the very organization of matter is a coefficient of its age. Four billion years ago a protein molecule was not a possibility anywhere in our surroundings. Matter had not sufficiently developed to produce this elaborate structure.

It took much longer for matter to be capable of the incredibly tight organization found in the human body. Nevertheless, over a period beginning with the emergence of life some one billion or more years ago, living beings did develop progressively more and more elaborate organization, more and more "complexification" or intensity of life. At a point where living organisms approximating the present human body finally were appearing, the first human soul is created by God, infused within a body on this globe of ours. This is, of course, a special act of God, for the creation of the human soul is always a special act of His, since the soul in its spirituality transcends the merely material. Moreover, God's freedom to create or not to create the universe at the start was of course absolute. But given the created and developing universe, it seems to compromise the divine wisdom to suggest that the creation of the first human soul was not called for at this point in a way analogous to that in which the creation of one's soul was called for when the germ cells from the bodies of his parents united. Is it possible to think that after five or ten billion years of elaboration, God might have simply let the ripeness of time go by? might have out of some whim simply failed to bring into being the first soul? To think this would seem to compromise God's fidelity to Himself. For we know enough of the story of an evolving cosmos to know that cosmic development had been pointing for billions upon billions of years to a certain fullness of time when material being had finally reached a point in which its spiritualization through a rational animal was possible. Because of this gigantic cosmic preparation, of which the preparation of the human ovum and sperm is only a kind of tiny echo, it seems quite proper and necessary to say that the whole cosmos gave birth to man. As a mother, it prepared the material for his body and, while not creating his human soul, presented him to the light of day.

The birth of man in the cosmos is striking evidence against cyclicism if further evidence is really needed. For here we have the cosmic processes terminating not in repetition but in its antithesis, the utterly unrepeatable and unique human person. And the cosmos matures by giving birth not merely to one, but to a riot of such persons. It showers itself with billions of induplicable consciousnesses, each profoundly alone in its isolation and yet integrated into a network of awarenesses, the social fabric, into which, indeed, each person must enter in order to come to a knowledge of himself and in which it becomes possible to achieve real communication—intimate union which does not deny utter difference but rather presupposes it.

But the story of the universe is not complete with the appearance of man, or even with the evolution of human society up to the present. As the universe continues its movement through time today, man is finding out more and more about his origins in the physical world in which he lives. We are living in an age in which man is identifying himself more and more with the material universe by pinpointing the network of connections between himself and the rest of God's material creation. Darwin's discoveries mark a stage in this movement whereby man finds himself more and more truly by finding the cosmos in which he lives. This movement is the contrary of that of Platonism and other ancient philosophies which drift away from a consideration of this world to a world of separated and supposedly "pure" ideas. The Platonic ideas are visually conceived in the sense that they are conceived by considering intellectual activity as analogous to vision and what we know intellectually by analogy with the objects of sight. *Idea* itself is the Greek cognate of the Latin *video* and of our English "vision." This reliance on vision yields a world of "objects" which are "clear and distinct," and quite directly produces the old Platonic and Aristotelian notion of "species," each cut off from one another, or, to use the more standard word signifying the same thing, "defined" one against the other. Darwin's discoveries represent a direct assault on this visualism, for in his account of the origin of species the old distinctness is lost in a blur of variants, potentially infinite in quantity and always at least incipient in the mere differentiation of individual from individual, although how far incipient depends somewhat on how far macroevolution dominates microevolution (if the two are effectively distinct at all).

The complaint has been made that the Darwinian view as against the Platonic focuses on this world and not on the world of spirit. Darwin is preoccupied with the story of the human body rather than of the human soul. Plato is interested in the soul and his "eternal verities." And what is the story of the body compared to my immortal soul? Yet there is something profoundly Christian in the Darwinian conception which is missing in the Platonic. For, although the Christian knows by his faith that the human soul is immortal, insistence upon the survival of the soul after death is not a distinguishing feature of divine revelation. Most of the Old Testament is silent about such survival, and in the New Testament, while this survival is supposed, it is enveloped in the strategically more important Christian doctrine of the resurrection of the body. Fascination with the survival of the soul is a mark of certain pagan philosophies. The resurrection of the body—born of this universe—is an article of faith distinctively Christian. Christian writers such as Father Robert W. Gleason in *The World to Come* have made this point, and the point needs making more frequently. The pagan may look forward to getting rid of his body and hence of this universe. The Christian does not look forward to this at all.

The world view which is opening out before us in our post-Darwinian world is thus one eminently congenial to a follower of Christ. For the universe in which we are finding man to be so profoundly at home—if at the same time so profoundly ill at ease, for we cannot deny this side of his experience although for want of time we must scant it here—is after all God's universe. Since elucidation of God's creation in a Christian framework is part of our mission as Christians, we Catholics face the major task of working out as full a cosmology as possible, one which takes advantage of all man knows about the universe as it really is—which is not always as we might have thought it to be or have wished it to be. For our task here we need to develop the positive habit of thinking of man within the full perspectives of time and space in which he exists in the cosmos—and that not just occasionally but regularly and habitually, in philosophy and theology as well as in other fields of knowledge.

But do not these perspectives derogate from the dignity of man? Are not you and I lost in these vast reaches of time? A conservative low figure for the age of the universe is five billion years. If we imagine that a moving-picture film had been made of the universe from a beginning five billion years ago up to today and that the film is shown in fast motion, speeded up so that the five-billion-year-long run is crowded into two hours, the period from the time when the first aquatic vertebrates evolved to the present day would be just over nine and a half minutes. The period of roughly five hundred thousand years from the time of the earliest known chipped stone tools to the present would be a little more than one-half second—a one-half second which would be the most important era of all. If this one-half second of film were itself slowed down to run two hours, the period from the first domestication of animals and plants to the present would occupy only about the last two minutes, and the period between the time of Our Lord and the present would take the last twenty-nine seconds.

This seems to make man impossibly small and insignificant. And so it does if we view him as though he were a tiny speck fetched from some realm of separated Platonic ideas and inserted into the vast reaches of time and space which the universe fills, or as a being coming into existence in an Aristotelian-type universe, an eternal datum cyclically organized. And yet if we view man as something which this universe has built up to out of these vast reaches of time and space, he is not insignificant at all. Before him, the prehuman universe is insignificant. For the supposition we have just made about viewing the universe in its early stages is an impossible one. The universe, for most of its early life, was one in which vision, and *a fortiori* photography, was an impossibility. For vision becomes possible only with living things, and the universe at first is a universe which will not tolerate any life at all.

One cannot validly imagine oneself as picking up by sight a universe which would destroy any seeing organ or indeed any living thing, even though at a later time when it has evolved to another state this same universe will produce sight. This would be like trying to imagine what a mass of molten steel in a blast furnace looks like to one sitting inside the molten steel. One can imagine various combinations of bright yellows and reds and blues and whites. But none really represent the actuality, which is simply and totally invisible—try sitting inside a mass of molten steel and see what you see—because it is simply intolerant of the conditions necessary for sight.

Because it is a universe which sight is unable to register, any attempt to understand the early universe starting from a visual image can never be fully successful. Any visual image we can form of it must give us only an analogue of the reality which of its very nature precluded all possibility of its being seen. However impressive it may be when we reconstruct it now in our imaginations and minds, and however agitated its hyperactivated molecules and masses, this was a dull and helpless universe at its start, intolerant of anything which might register even the fact that it was there. With the advent of man, this fact is registered. The universe is visible in time only from the end of time near ourselves. Its beginning is not intelligible, or even visible, except from our portal of the tunnel of time out of which man emerges. And thus the reconstruction of the brute facts of four or five billion—perhaps ten billion—years ago in man's mind today is more wonderful and impressive than the original facts themselves. Against the backdrop of the infrahuman universe which has given him birth, man remains more impressive than the rest of this universe. For he, as nothing before him, really includes it all. It comes to life and fruition in him.

Even if this were not so, it is against this cosmic backdrop that man must be viewed and, indeed, that God's Providence and revelation to man must be conceived. Against this backdrop the Incarnation took place. Any educated man, and much more any Catholic educator, must view himself and all mankind and God's action in this cosmic scene, and must do so not occasionally but habitually. A Christ projected by our imaginations, consciously or subconsciously, into any universe other than this real one is to that extent unreal. Only with as full as possible an understanding of the universe as it actually has been and is can we hope to realize effectively, with His grace, what is the meaning of His Incarnation in this evolving creation and in this always more and more closely knit human society which through Him was brought into being and through Him and with Him and in Him is being brought to its mysterious fruition.

NOTES ON THE
CONTRIBUTORS

JAMES COLLINS, Ph.D., Professor of Philosophy at St. Louis University, is one of the leading Catholic philosophers of the United States. He is a regular contributor to numerous learned journals and the author of several books. His most recent publications are *God in Modern Philosophy* and a revised and bibliographically updated edition of his book *The Existentialists: A Critical Study.*

ROBERT W. GLEASON, S.J., Ph.D., S.T.D., is Chairman of the Departments of Theology and Religious Education at Fordham University. He has studied here and abroad and lectured widely at congresses and institutes in Spain and Italy. His articles in *Thought, Irish Theological Quarterly, Australian Catholic Record, Clergy Review* of England and in most of the theological journals in English-speaking countries have been cited in many international reviews. He is the author of *The World to Come, Christ and the Christian,* and co-author of *Counselling the Catholic.*

VINCENT C. HOPKINS, S.J., S.T.L., Ph.D., is Associate Professor of History at Fordham University. He formerly lectured on Jurisprudence in the School of Law at Fordham University, and was the editor of *The Catholic Encyclopedia Supplement.* He is the author of *Dred Scott's Case* and of various articles in learned periodicals.

WALTER J. ONG, S.J., S.T.L., Ph.D., Professor of English at St. Louis University, has lectured and published widely in the United States and Europe on both Renaissance and contemporary literature and civilization. Two recent books of his, *Ramus, Method, and the Decay of Dialogue* and *Ramus and Talon Inventory,* were the product of four years of research work in Europe, two of these years as a Guggenheim Fellow.

Two other recent books of his are *Frontiers in American Catholicism* and *American Catholic Crossroads*.

ALEXANDER WOLSKY, Ph.D., Professor of Experimental Embryology in the Graduate School of Fordham University, formerly served as principal scientific officer for the United Nations Educational, Scientific and Cultural Organization, and was a Professor of Budapest University and Director of the Hungarian Biological Institute in Tihany. He is the author of some eighty research publications on developmental physiology and physiological genetics, and is often quoted in textbooks on these subjects. A member of numerous learned societies here and abroad (Great Britain, Germany, India), he was a Rockefeller Fellow in 1935–1936, and had research and travel grants from Sweden and the prewar government of Hungary.

INDEX